Stained Glass Sidewalks

By Tim Walter

Learn more about this book
and its author by visiting our website:
www.overboardminsitries.com

This book is also available as an ebook,
visit www.overboardministries.com for details.

Contents

Dedication

I dedicate this book to the hidden evangelists of the world that nobody has ever heard of. Those who never can share their stories in a book. Those deep in the jungles, in the mountains, in the underground churches, in the areas of intense persecution. May this book honor the sacrifices you all make in sharing the gospel with others. I look forward to meeting you one day in Glory, and to see you all receive the many rewards of your labors. You all live for the audience of One...and in the end, that is all that is needed.

Prologue

Stained glass sidewalks—picture that in your mind for a minute. I doubt you've ever seen a sidewalk made of stained glass. I know I haven't. Stained glass is beautiful, colorful, and majestic. Historically, stained glass was often used to tell the gospel story to those who could not read. Because only the "educated clergy" could read and write, it was artists who told the Bible stories through stained glass, bringing the God of the Bible to the peasant, the cobbler, and the beggar.

Stained glass has a rich history of bringing the greatest news in the world to the common person through its beauty and color. It takes simple light from the outside a building, makes it into a plethora of colors that creates a window into a story, and brings new, bright perspective to ordinary things. Its whole purpose is to magnify the beauty of something else, whether it be a cathedral, church, library, or wherever it is found.

I visited St. Patrick's Cathedral in Ireland, and Notre Dame in France. Both had stained glass within them, and as I gazed upon those massive windows and the beauty of the light that shined through them, I could not help but ponder the beauty and majesty of God. In those massive cathedrals, gazing at the beauty of the stained glass, I was reminded of how big and beautiful God is, and how small I am.

Then there are sidewalks. There is nothing too special about them at all; common, everywhere, filled with cracks and signs of wear and tear over years of use. Here in the Northwest, many of them are broken up by the massive roots of trees that grow beneath them. Sidewalks are for the common person, going about life. They are meant to connect us with people and places. To my knowledge, nobody has ever traveled long distances to see the beauty and grandeur of a sidewalk.

Sidewalks have a special meaning for me, as they have provided me hours upon hours of time with my family on our family walks. We take a two-and-a-half mile walk around our neighborhood every day. That's 912 miles of walking on sidewalks a year for me and my family. At 45 minutes a walk, that adds up to 274 hours of time spent walking and talking with my wife and kids. I've had some amazing conversations about God with my kids on those walks. Sidewalks have taken on a new meaning for me. In a way, sidewalks have become like church. Sidewalks are also where I spend my days talking to people about the gospel.

I titled this book *Stained Glass Sidewalks* because I believe that the gospel is the most beautiful and majestic message in the world. It is like stained glass in its beauty and grandeur. I believe the gospel is also practical, meant for us to be lived out here and now, and it's often messy and filled with cracks, much like sidewalks. Stained glass by itself is unapproachable, distant, and seemingly removed from us, much like God. The stained-glass-sidewalk gospel is meant to show us our inability to connect with the Holy God of the Bible because of our sin, and the good news that through His grace and humility, He came down to the sidewalk for us. When Jesus came to this earth, He gave us an example to follow. He showed us how the

Divine made Himself available and approachable to us. He could have stayed in the stained glass case we often ascribe to God, but He did not; He humbled himself and walked the "sidewalks" of Israel 2,000 years ago.

As Christians we need to have a stained-glass-sidewalk gospel: a gospel that admires and worships the majesty of God, while at the same time bringing that beautiful message everywhere we go. The sidewalks of every believer might look different. It could be your workplace, it could be your family, it could be your morning walk. We have a calling to be like stained glass, allowing the love and grace of God to shine through us as we walk the sidewalks of our lives. We must show and tell others of the One who saves.

As you read this book, my hope is that these stories will help you to see two things. First, I hope you will see the beauty and majesty of God. Like stained glass, He is beautiful, bright, and majestic. He is often indescribable by human words. Second, I hope you will see that the gospel is meant for the sidewalks of life. The gospel, at the core, is about the majestic God becoming meek for our sake. He came down for us. It is a message that needs to go with us wherever we are, no matter if that sidewalk is smooth or bumpy, new or old. The gospel must be lived out in a real and tangible way, despite all our flaws and weaknesses.

***

My office in the center of downtown Salem is a humble little office, neatly wedged between a cobbler's store and a florist. It has a kind of nostalgic feel to it being located there, and it sits right across the street from the bus station, smack dab in the middle of our city. Go to the right and you can have a great cup of coffee at the local coffee shop; go to the left and you can hit the mall to do some shopping. Kitty-corner to it is the courthouse and police station, which sit across from the downtown theater and a nice Italian restaurant. Across the street at the bus station, you can step into a world riddled with homeless people and drug-addicted teens.

Yes, that little office is located in the crossroads of various worldviews, and it is no wonder the Lord gave us this oasis in the storm of it all. It is a place you would hardly call an office, as it is literally just a back room of the florist next door who kindly allows us to rent it. It used to be a Christian Science reading room, and through a miraculous event too long to be told in this prologue, the Lord laid in our laps the opportunity to rent it after they moved out. To the passerby, the office seems like an ordinary run-of-the mill storefront office, but to me and to many others, it is much more than that. True, there is nothing special or magical about the office itself, but there is something extraordinary and supernatural about the God who uses that office for His purposes.

You see, God has used the ministry that flows out of that little office to reach our city for the gospel, and continues to do so to this day. This book is a collection of stories that have come as a result of ministry happening out of that office.

As I was thinking one day of some things that God has done out of this little office, I began to recall story after story, some good, some bad, all amazing. I started to write notes of some of my favorite stories, and before I knew it, this book came into being. Like all stories, sometimes the details are fuzzy, though I tried my best to make sure I stayed true to each one. One of the ways I did that was by contacting many of the people you will meet in this book, relaying the story, and asking them if they remembered it the same.

The people in these stories are real. This is not a philosophical book about doctrine, but a collection of stories that actually took place, in real time, with real people. Most of the names are the real names of the people, but some out of humility have asked their names not to be mentioned, so I have switched names in a few instances. Those that don't have names are simply because I have forgotten the names of the people within those stories.

I think this book is kind of like the Blockbuster movie stores we used to have. Remember the fun of walking into a movie store, finding your favorite section, and seeing what movies they had? Just like movies come in different genres, so do these stories. Some are adventure, filled with the twists and turns that God brings us on. Some are mysteries, where we see God's ways often are simply things we were never meant to know. Some are drama, filled with people, their issues, their struggles, and their victories, and how God fits into it all. Some are action, where we see the living God moving, and actually doing things today. Some are comedy, filled with the humor of making mistakes, learning from them, and often laughing at the funny way God sometimes does things. Some are sci-fi, being simply weird and "out of this world." Some are horror, revealing the tragedy that comes when people reject the gospel.

But all these stories are part of a great saga of how a Holy God continues to reach out to sinful people, undeserving of His grace and mercies. In the end, these stories collectively are a biography about God. These are His stories. He is the one involved in the orchestrating of them and the glory goes to Him. I write this book simply to point people to Him who is the great Author of salvation. These are stories I hope will encourage people to look to Jesus. If any story in this book points you to pursue Jesus more, then it was well worth my time and effort to write it.

I often have pondered the meaning of the Scripture in John 21:25: *"And there are also many other things which Jesus did, which if they were written in detail, I suppose that even the world itself would not contain the books which were written."* Through the process of writing this book, I think I caught a glimpse of what John meant. I simply cannot write about all the stories the Lord has done out of that little office downtown. Everyone involved with Gospel Focus could write books, as well, remembering all God has done.

To narrow it down to a few stories has been both easy, in that there are just so many stories to select from, and difficult, in deciding which ones I wanted to put in this little book. I tried to choose stories that cover a whole range of situations that often come during evangelism. Some are simply stories of what God does when like-minded people gather. Yes, the stories coming out of that office could fill all the libraries of the world with stories similar to what you are about to read.

I hope this little book encourages you in your walk with Jesus. I hope it challenges you to share the gospel.

I hope it reminds you that we have a living God, who still does amazing things, and is still involved with our lives. I hope it reminds you that following Jesus is truly the most exciting, life-giving adventure one can begin. Lastly, I hope that every page of this book points to the cross and the empty tomb. To Him be all the glory. Thanks for reading.

A Lunch I'll Never Forget

Jesus answered and said to him, "Truly, truly, I say to you, unless one is born again, he cannot see the kingdom of God."– John 3:3

Every three months, we have a new Discipleship Training School (DTS) that begins at our YWAM campus. It is always an exciting time as new students from all across the globe meet and embark on a five-month journey of growing closer to Jesus, and doing missions work. During each session of school, these students get to spend an afternoon a week with our ministry doing evangelism.

As I mentioned, the students come from all over the globe, and one of the students was a young man named Recky, who was from Papua New Guinea. I connected with him right away as he was a rugby player, and since I used to play, it was a natural point of connection. We had only taken the students of this school out to do evangelism a few times, so I did not know him too well yet, and I had never done evangelism with him. The school leader approached me one day and asked me if I would talk to Recky, as she did not think he was doing well. Of course I said, "Sure."

I was grabbing lunch one day and noticed that Recky was sitting by himself eating lunch at a picnic table. I sensed a nudging to go sit with him and talk. "How are you doing, man?"

"Okay, Tim...I guess. It's all good."

I could tell he was not really being honest with me, so I pressed him a bit and asked him, "Recky, how's the school going?"

He paused, "It's okay, I guess...but I am really confused." I asked him to explain what he meant, and in a nutshell he shared how even though he liked all the teachings and loved his classmates, he just couldn't really understand what was being taught, or what in the world he was even doing here. "You know, my dad sent me here to 'set me on the right path,'" he told me. "I don't even know what that path is."

I asked him about his life story, and he shared how he grew up in a tribal culture, had multiple mothers, and was kind of a party animal. His dad was a tribal chief and sent him to Salem to "get things in order." His dad had sent other kids to YWAM schools before or something like that and it had a positive impact on them, so he sent Recky to Salem, Oregon. No idea why here, exactly, but Recky was here.

After listening to his story, I could tell his greatest aspiration in life was to live up to his father's and family's expectations, and that was directly affecting how he approached God. I asked him if he knew what the gospel was, and to the best of his ability he shared what he believed it to be, but it was far from the true gospel.

"Recky, may I share the gospel with you? I want you to know that before I do, I am going to ask you if you would like to respond to what I'm about to tell you. It's a dangerous thing that I am about to share with you, but it is also the most wonderful thing. Dangerous in that it will offend you, and demand all of your life. Wonderful, in that the love of God is at the core of it." He agreed.

I shared the gospel with him and then asked him what he thought. He had tears in his eyes, and he said, "Tim, I want that. How do I 'do' that?" I then shared with him and highlighted faith, righteousness, and that salvation was a gift of God's grace to be received and that he could do nothing to earn it. And with that, Recky bowed his head, repented of his sins and trusted in Christ for salvation. A few weeks later, I had the privilege to be asked to baptize him along with his school leader. They even threw him a "birthday party" with his favorite food...grilled chicken! It was a special time.

Recky was a different guy the rest of the school. His evangelism exploded, because now it was his experience with God, not just a message he was told was important. Recky went on to attend more schools in YWAM, and began doing medical ministries in his native land.

I learned so much from that day. I learned that God is the master chess player. For some reason, His will was for a guy to come all the way across the planet to meet Jesus. I learned that evangelism is not something that we can simply turn the switch on and off. I was not downtown in our office that day Recky came to Christ, I was at our YWAM campus; but evangelism does not stop when you leave the office. I learned that many people, though hearing good teachings, and being involved in Christian activity, still need their hearts and eyes opened before they can understand what they are hearing, and this can only come through the work of the Holy Spirit.

I serve in a wonderful mission which willingly takes on students who don't even know Jesus, to reach them with the gospel. On the path of salvation, God puts many people into an individual's life to point them to Jesus. Recky had not only me in his life, he had his school staff and leaders, and his fellow students, who all played an important part in him making that decision over lunch.

Lastly, I learned from Recky that when we truly realize who we are, and what Christ did for us, then we cannot help but share with others through our time and talents. Recky went on to be a blessing to many, and that was because of his recognition of the blessing that he experienced through his faith in Jesus Christ. The day Recky placed his faith in Christ was a wonderful day, and that lunch will always be a lunch I will never forget.

Questions to Ponder

1. Do you tend to "turn on" and "turn off" evangelism rather than simply let it be who you are?

2. How sensitive are you to the nudging the Holy Spirit may give you when He is asking you to speak to a person specifically?

3. Why do so many people find it hard to accept the grace of God in salvation, and desire to "prove their worth" to God?

A Person and a Cross

Then Jesus said to His disciples, "If anyone wishes to come after Me, let him deny himself, and take up his cross, and follow Me." – Matthew 16:24

As we walked through the main green quad of the university, you would have thought we just landed in a saucer from outer space the way people were looking at us. We could feel the looks, as if the eyes of people were fixed right on us. Some were looks of curiosity, others were looks of confusion, and some were looks of annoyance. It's not every day that you see a big group of people silently walking through your college campus dragging a wooden cross, so I could totally understand the looks we were receiving.

We were doing our "Crosswalk" outreach at one of the universities in our city that day. Crosswalk is always a very powerful and solemn time. We simply drag a wooden cross in silence, the whole time reflecting on what Christ did for us, and interceding in prayer for those who see us. If you've never done a "Crosswalk," I highly encourage you to do it, as it is a very humbling way to spend your day. One of the rules we have is that you must stay silent, as Christ was silent in His shame. Many times this is hard to do, especially when an occasional person yells out some rude profanity or humiliating words. Of course, if anyone walked up to us and politely inquired as to what we were doing, we would tell them, but we tried to keep it a time of solitary reflection.

One of the leaders of our group had been a student at this university years prior. Before we left our office that morning, she asked for prayer as she knew what we were going to do. As each person dragged the cross for a few minutes and then passed it onto the next, it was Monica's turn. She took it up and began to walk. I was behind her a few yards back, just praying for her as she carried the cross and praying for those watching.

Now typically, people carry the cross for about three minutes or so, but Monica signaled for us to take the cross only a minute or so after she started to drag it. I went up to take it from her and saw the tears in her eyes. "I need to sit down. I need a moment." Her eyes were filled with tears, and she took a seat on a rock nearby and just began to cry. We gave her a few minutes to herself and then walked over to her to ask her how she was doing.

"I'm fine...it's just that when I was carrying the cross I was remembering the person I used to be when I was a student here, the things I used to do, and now, here I am a totally different person. I'm just so grateful for what Jesus has done in my life, and that He loved me when I was the type of person I used to be. This is such a good, but hard, thing for me to do." We then had a great discussion on the saving power of Jesus, His grace in our lives, and how grateful we all were. Monica smiled, gave us all a hug, and then continued on with the group, carrying the cross proudly in a place she once would have scorned it.

I learned that day that the cross is a very personal thing. The group had a great time dragging that cross, but for Monica, it was a truly powerful time because it was so personal. That's the gospel, isn't it? It is a personal message we hear, and a personal experience we have with Christ. I learned that it is important to recall and reflect on who we once were, in order to better appreciate who we are and have become through Christ. The reason that the Crosswalk was so powerful for Monica was because it reminded her of the darkness of her life before Christ, which highlighted the brightness of her life now in Christ.

The cross will always be foolishness to the world and to the proud of heart. The looks and comments we got from people that day in some cases were rude, demeaning, and embarrassing. The cross does that. It divides. It confronts. It strips away all sense of worthiness and ego. It simply does what it was meant to do: kill. It kills our pride, self-righteousness, and ego. Most importantly, it kills the sin that once separated us from God. It was amazing for me that day to see the beauty of the cross magnified in the life of a person. Monica went on to be an influential mover and shaker in our city with her church and with an organization dedicated to helping bring Christ into all spheres of society.

Questions to Ponder

1. How are you "bearing your cross" for Christ today?

2. Why is it important for you to reflect on who you were before you knew Christ?

3. Why is it so important to not just know that Jesus died for the sins of the world, but also for your own sins?

A Trip Down Memory Lane

I shall remember the deeds of the Lord; surely I will remember Thy wonders of old. – Psalm 77:11

As the bus traveled from stop to stop, I knew that I needed to just get over my fear and stand up and share the gospel. As the high schoolers who were with me awkwardly waited for something to happen, I said a silent prayer to the tune of, "Lord Jesus, I am scared right now and have no idea how this is going to go, but please use me right now for Your glory." I once again decided to lead by example when I told the group of high schoolers that I would be the first person to share. Why did I do that?

In the summer, we often brought youth groups on our city buses to do proclamation evangelism. Standing up in a bus and sharing the gospel is one of those experiences that will crucify your flesh and ego in so many ways. This day was nothing different. There is probably no more intimidating thing to do, to be honest. *What will the captive audience think? Will I be told to leave the bus? Is this the best way to share the gospel? Will people think I'm some weird doomsday guy?* The fears, doubts, and excuses welled up inside me as to why I should not do it. *Tim, just stand up and share,* I heard in my mind and felt in my heart.

So, like a scared kid jumping off a diving board for his first time, I took the plunge and stood up, and for the next few minutes shared the gospel. Though my heart was beating a thousand beats a minute, and some people were glaring at me with discontent at what they were hearing, I managed to make it through to the end. As I sat down, I looked back at the high schoolers who were with me, and before I knew it, one stood up and shared. The others then began to talk to the people they were sitting next to, and the bus was filled with the sounds of conversations. The gospel was being shared literally all over the bus! It was amazing.

As we approached the bus station after what was about a 30-minute round trip, I noticed the last few miles the bus driver kept looking back at me through the mirror. *Uh-oh, I bet he is going to tell me to get off the bus, or something like that*, I thought. I awkwardly tried to avoid eye contact, but his glance was like a tractor beam, and I kept finding myself staring at him. We finally got to the bus station, and as people were getting off the bus, the driver stood up and motioned to me to come to the front. *Here we go*, I thought. *I was probably on camera, and will end up getting sued or something like that.* I was fully expecting to be read the riot act by the driver.

I remember as I walked toward him, I thought that he had the look of a Russian. After living in Russia for many years, I can often pick them out from a crowd. As I stood before him, he introduced himself in a very strong Russian accent. "Hi, my name is Yuri." *I knew it!* "Do you normally go on to people's buses and preach?"

A bit taken aback by his kind demeanor and question, I told him not too often, but only occasionally. He then asked me to sit down, and he shut the bus door. It was only me and the high school group who were with me on the bus at this point. He began to tell his story.

"I grew up in Ukraine (so he wasn't Russian after all, but I was close!) under the strong hand of the communist Soviet Union. I was raised in a Christian home, but because of communism, we were not allowed to worship freely at all." At this point, he had our attention. As he continued, you could see the emotion begin to well up within him. "I remember the day communism fell, and the first thing my friends and I did was go onto the subway cars and preach the gospel." As he said that, his eyes filled with water and a tear fell on the side of his face. "I immigrated to the United States thirty years ago, and this is the first time I have ever seen Christians do what you're doing today. Thirty years. Thank you for preaching on my bus today. We need more people to do what you did today. Anytime you want to preach the gospel on a bus, come find mine. As a matter of fact, I'd like to join you sometime when I retire."

After I gave him a big hug and thanked him for sharing, I got off the bus and had a tremendous time debriefing our time on Yuri's bus with the high school students. The lesson I learned that day was that sometimes, the preaching of the gospel is a tremendous encouragement to others who see it happening. We often take for granted the things we assume are normal, like the freedom to share the gospel in the open. Yuri was brought down memory lane that day, to a time when he used to preach the gospel because he realized how to take advantage of the freedom to do so, since it had for so long been taken from him under communism.

Yuri taught me that day to never, ever take for granted the freedom we have here in the States to openly proclaim the name of Jesus. Yuri reminded us all by those tears in his eyes, and the emotion in his voice, that the treasure of the gospel is something to be shared. We have since had to stop preaching on our city buses. We began to do it so much, the city began to get complaints from people. We always did it in love with grace, but I guess sometimes things like that happen. I miss those days, and will never forget the amazing times we had on those buses.

Questions to Ponder

1. How are you using the freedom you have to share the gospel with others?

2. Are there things you have taken for granted in your walk with Christ?

3. In what ways can you be an encouragement to other believers today?

A Very Awkward Office Visit

And Jesus asked him, "What is your name?" And he said, "Legion"; for many demons had entered him. – Luke 8:30

Have you ever been trying to do a math problem, and things just don't seem to add up? You know the formula, you go over and over it, but for some reasons, something is off and you just can't seem to place your finger on it?

It had been a good morning doing evangelism and Shane and I were debriefing over a cup of coffee in our office. We were just getting ready to head out when a lady approached our door. This happens all the time, as our office is located in the center of the city across from the bus station, and lots of people will stop by. That creates some great opportunities to share the gospel, but it has also placed us in some very uncomfortable situations at times. Whether it be homeless people coming in asking for food or money, well-intentioned people trying to find out more about our ministry, or people from out of town simply asking for directions, the location of our office keeps us on our toes with walking that fine balance beam of knowing who to help, and how to help.

On this day, the lady came in and began to ask simple questions about our ministry. At first she seemed very sincere and interested in getting involved. She was a bit older, and talked about how she trusted in Christ back in the 70s during the "Jesus Movement." Her demeanor was friendly, but something just did not seem right about her. As she began to talk more, something was not adding up. Some of the things she was saying were a bit "off" when it comes to what you would hear a typical believer say.

As she talked, Shane and I glanced at each other a time or two. We both were thinking the same thing, and we both began to pray in our spirits for wisdom. Shane was actually supposed to be leaving as he had another appointment, but the moment this lady began to talk to us he felt that he needed to stay back with me. This is a safeguard "rule" we have in our ministry that we never have a male and female alone in the office together anyway, so I knew he would be hanging back, but I did not know that he was also feeling led by the Spirit to do so.

Many times, I equate conversations with someone bringing their car in to a mechanic. I typically ask a few "diagnostic" questions to see where they are in their understanding of who God is, and the gospel. I needed to find out what "issue" we were dealing with here. I needed to figure out where this lady stood spiritually and theologically, so I asked her two very simple questions. I asked her if she believed Jesus was God and what she understood the gospel to be. It was then that things got weird.

"It's the pigtails, isn't it?!" she loudly said to us. I looked at Shane, and we each had a puzzled look on our face. "It's the pigtails! You're like all the rest of them!" she said again as she stood up. I've never been a detail person, but at this point I noticed she actually had pigtails in her hair, and she was pointing at them. I could feel a demonic presence in the room. It was very real and right there. Her eyes even took on a new look. It's hard to explain, but once you have experienced it, there is no doubt when you're around it.

She continued to tell us we "were like the rest of them" and that "we did not know the gospel." She went on a rant that we did not know the true gospel, and that we were deceived like "the rest of them." I tried a few times to interrupt her kindly with a statement or a question, but it was no use. I remember praying, "Lord, what do we do?" Then I decided to ask her name again.

"I told you, my name is Dianne!"

She may have not known it, but I was talking to the demon she had within her when I asked that. I had hoped the demon would say its name, but it did not. I do not have much experience at all in demonic deliverance-type ministry, so I was just doing what I see Jesus and the apostles do when confronted by demonic forces in the scriptures. Finally she opened our door to leave, turned around and told us that one day we would know the real gospel and that we were fake.

Then something very odd happened. First, the atmosphere of the room simply changed. It became somehow "lighter." The other thing was, Shane was drinking a cup of coffee, and at the exact moment the lady shut the door, the bottom of his Styrofoam coffee cup fell out and his coffee spilled all over him! It was one of the weirdest things I've ever seen. It was as if someone literally just pulled out the bottom of his coffee cup.

I don't want to go on a witch hunt, and sure, maybe the Styrofoam cup's bottom was faulty, and it just so happened to fall out at that exact time, but never in my years of following Jesus had something that odd happened. Coincidence? I don't know. A demon doing some weird thing to the cup? I don't know. One thing is for sure though, when the lady left the office, we felt "something" leave with her as well.

Oftentimes, people can say churchy types of things, but be living in darkness. This lady came in sharing her "testimony" and actually appeared to be interested in our ministry. I learned that discernment is a powerful thing when talking to someone. Shane and I both had a feeling that something was "off" when this lady began to speak, and that was because the Holy Spirit was giving us discernment. The forces of darkness cannot even compare to the power of God. Despite the awkwardness of that whole situation, we had nothing to fear because the Holy Spirit lives within us.

I also learned once again that the demonic world is indeed very real, and in our western world we fail to acknowledge that so much of the time. Lastly, I learned that the easiest way to "stir" up darkness in the world is to proclaim the simple gospel. When we asked her about the gospel and Jesus, that is when the demon seemed to manifest. I was reminded that Jesus died for people like this lady, and that despite the demonic influence in her life, she needed to hear the gospel about the love and grace of God.

Questions to Ponder

1. How sensitive do you think you are to the leadings of the Holy Spirit in your life?

2. Why is it important to exercise spiritual discernment as a believer?

3. What are some ways you can measure a crazy experience and whether or not it is something the enemy is behind?

A Very Sad Conversation

Since by works of the Law shall no flesh be justified. –
Galatians 2:16b

It was a hot summer day, and we were downtown at the city market doing evangelism. It is a great place to share the gospel. There are tent vendors everywhere, people walking about buying food and drinks, plenty of local produce, and an all-around lighthearted atmosphere. I love doing evangelism in those settings.

As I drank my ice-cold lemonade, which had become a staple for me during the hot summertime, I noticed an elderly gentleman approaching me. He wore a WWII veteran hat, and seemed to just be strolling around casually. "Do you have a minute for a conversation? " I asked him.

"A minute? My wife is in the market shopping, I have hours!" he said. We both laughed, and commiserated with each other on how both our wives seem to disappear into the "Bermuda Triangle" any time they go shopping.

I commented on his WWII veteran's hat. "Where did you serve?" I asked him.

"I was in the South Pacific. Marine Corps."

I then told him about my grandfather being in the war in the South Pacific, and that led to us talking about his story for the next thirty minutes. If there ever was a nicer man, I never knew one. If there ever was a guy who looked like he was the poster child for every Norman Rockwell painting ever made, it was him. Not only was he a WWII veteran, but he also served in the Korean War, started his own business, was involved in all sorts of charity work, had kids, grandkids, a lovely wife, and the list could go on. He was simply a good guy.

As we continued to talk, I knew it was time for me to begin to transition the conversation to the gospel. I asked him what he believed about God, and he politely replied, "Oh, I'm not religious, I don't believe in any of that stuff." I asked him a bunch of questions, trying to figure out how he came to where he was at in his spiritual journey. I then asked him if he had ever heard the gospel, and if I could share it with him.

He looked around for his wife, which I interpreted as maybe a lifeline for him to find a way out of the conversation, but since he could not find her he told me, "Sure." I shared the gospel, and focused primarily on the aspect of us all being sinners, and that before a Holy God we actually are not good at all. I tried every illustration I could conjure up to try and get the point across to him that he needed a Savior, and that despite all his accomplishments in life, on Judgment Day they would all be worthless without Christ.

After I finished he looked at me and said, "I appreciate what you're trying to do here, I really do, but it's just not for me. And if this heaven and hell thing is for real, I think I'll turn out okay, after all the good things I've done." He politely shook my hand, and walked off to go find his wife in the sea of people at the market.

As he walked away, my heart sank. I remember literally feeling a bit sick to my stomach at what had just happened. It was one of the saddest conversations I have ever had. I wanted to shake the guy, and get him to see what he was rejecting. Here was a guy who not only had it all in life, but did it all as well. And yet, he had absolutely no interest in the only One who truly matters. He had no interest in a God who saves. He had no interest in salvation. And the saddest part about it all, is he was such a nice guy. I felt so badly for him, because I knew he was trusting in his own righteousness, not in the righteousness of Christ.

The sad truth is that the road to hell is filled with people just like that guy: well-meaning, kind-hearted, loving people. But the Scriptures are clear that we all need a Savior. I learned in that conversation that I simply have no idea the mystery of how the Spirit of God works on some people, and not on others. I tried everything to get him to understand, but nothing seemed to work. I could not get through to him. Why didn't the Lord open his heart? Or why didn't he open his heart? I have no idea. Some things of the Lord will always remain a mystery to us. Theological explanation is many times just a smokescreen to cover the simple fact that we have no idea how the Holy Spirit works at times.

I learned that many people appear humble on the outside, but inside they are filled with a pride that is an offense to Jesus. This was exactly this man's issue. He was so proud of himself, he saw no need for a Savior in his life. As the old cliché states, you can truly never judge a book by its cover. Here was a guy who in every way, shape, and form seemed to have it all together, and yet inside he was lost, separated from God, and full of pride. I often think of that nice old man and wonder if he is still around. I hope and pray that somehow, in the mystery of God's will and man's choice, he surrendered his pride to the One who became humble to save nice guys like him.

Questions to Ponder

1. How comfortable are you speaking with "good people" about their need of a Savior?

2. How can you share the gospel with "good people" in truth and love?

3. Why is it so important to have a biblical perspective on the true condition of a person's soul?

An Atheist and a Christian Meet at a Coffin

Conduct yourselves with wisdom toward outsiders, making the most of the opportunity. – Colossians 4:5

I stood with my coffee next to the six-foot wooden coffin on the college green, once again wondering what I had gotten myself into with this crazy idea. As people walked by me, the looks on their faces showed a mix of curiosity, confusion, disdain, and even concern. Sure, a big wooden coffin like the one I was standing next to would fit in with a set design for an old western, but on a college campus? One thing is for sure, it stuck out like a sore thumb, and it was too late to back out now. The coffin itself was too big for me to carry alone, and as I pondered that, I asked myself why Ryan hadn't made it smaller!

A few weeks prior I had asked my friend, Ryan, who is a jack of all trades, if he would build us a coffin to use for evangelism. As always, he was excited by the idea and went straight to work. Ryan is probably one of the only friends I have who is always ready to try anything to reach people for Jesus, no matter how weird it may seem. The type of friend who you can always blame for bad ideas if the one you had does not work out right. Those are good friends, too.

As I mentioned, he is a jack of all trades, and can basically build, fix, or create anything. Everything Ryan does is done well, and the coffin was no exception. The only problem was, the coffin was big enough for Goliath to fit in, which made it a bit tough to take places. The coffin actually has contributed to a few of our staff injuring themselves while carrying it. Maybe one day we will cut it in half, but that's down the line, I guess.

For now, we are stuck with a coffin that can honestly serve many purposes. It can be used for a great table, or if a flood happens it can be used as a lifeboat for at least eight people to fit in. As I stood by the coffin, I prayed a simple prayer. "Lord, here I am next to this coffin. I feel awkward, and maybe even a bit morbid. But I think you want me to do this, so please, draw people to you today."

The day started off with great conversations. As a matter of fact, there was not a minute's rest as I was constantly engaged with people. As the morning drew on, and I had a break to grab another cup of coffee, a young man approached me with a smile on his face and he said, "What in the world is this?"

I introduced myself, and shared with him that I was a Christian guy who wanted to talk to people about their beliefs on what they think happens when you die. "Cool, I'm down for a conversation. My name is David, and I'm an atheist, so this will be a good one."

Over the next hour, David and I had a fantastic conversation. He was a very smart guy, and was studying to be a physicist, if that tells you anything about his intellect. As we came to the end of our conversation, David said, "You know, I have to be honest. When I saw you out here next to this coffin I was pretty excited to come over here and destroy your arguments piece by piece. I've done that with so many Christians, it's almost fun. But you're a different type of Christian. You're not the 'typical evangelical.' To be honest, you did not use the same arguments I often hear, and you actually bring up some good counter points and questions, man." Chuckling, he said, "You're a Christian who can actually think critically. I appreciate that."

I responded to him, "Hey man, thanks for the kind words. To be fair, you're not the 'typical atheist' either. You asked me some good questions, and brought up some great points as well. It's nice talking to an atheist who doesn't want to just argue with me. You open for coffee sometime?"

"Absolutely, man, here's my number." David and I became good friends, and he has come to be a person I respect very much. For a while, we would meet at Denny's for coffee, and have a tennis match of worldview discussions. He is still an atheist, and I pray someday he will come to know Christ. David has been on our ministry podcast in the past, and has partaken in many discussions over the years.

When I think about my first conversation with David, I learn a lot of things. People appreciate sincerity, no matter how crazy you may seem. When David saw me standing by a coffin, he didn't just see a weird guy who had an obsession with death, he saw a sincere Christian wanting to seriously discuss his beliefs. I learned that we can have great discussions with people, do evangelism, and still be friends with those to whom we are witnessing. David is a friend, and even though our worldviews are different, our respect and appreciation for each other has only grown over time.

I learned that one of the most effective ways to witness to people is through asking questions, and listening. I learned that oftentimes, the Lord will bring a guy like David into your life to remind you that we cannot broad-stroke people into categories. We are all individuals. David had some preconceived notions about Christians, as I had a few about atheists. Both of us were reminded that a group is nothing more than a collection of individuals, all with their own system of beliefs held within the group they belong to. We need to take time to get to know the individual, not just label the individual based on the "group" they adhere to. Jesus died for the whole world, and He died for each individual within the whole world.

Questions to Ponder

1. Do you find yourself labeling people into categories rather than looking at them as individuals and as Christ sees them?

2. How sincere would you say you are in your Christian witness? Do people see sincerity in you?

3. How willing would you say you are in wanting to know others' beliefs?

Carolizing

I will sing to the Lord, because He has dealt bountifully with me. – Psalm 13:6

When it comes to evangelism, I've always gone by the theory of "throw spaghetti on the wall and see what sticks." In other words, I like to try anything that will allow me the opportunity to talk to people about Jesus. Sometimes those ideas crash and burn quickly, and other times they seem to stick, and work great.

One of these ideas dawned upon me a few years back as Christmas was approaching. I was organizing a group of people to go Christmas caroling to get us in the festive mood. I've always been a fan of old-school, simple fun like that. One of my favorite things is taking my younger kids out with me to go caroling in our neighborhood. I say younger, because at some point as my kids have grown older they realize that caroling is not that cool, and leave me to the wolves.

As I was reading through the old carols I had often sung in church as a kid, I could not help but notice how theologically rich they were. Songs like "O Holy Night," "What Child is This," and "Oh Come All Ye Faithful" are full of solid, amazing theology. *These are sermons in themselves,* I thought to myself. Then, I began to think of how caroling could be a great way to not just sing and bring Christmas cheer, but also to do evangelism. Do evangelism, while singing carols. Call it "carolizing."

And just like that, I was putting together a collection of carols, along with a simple gospel message that would go with each one. The idea was simple. Sing a carol, then have someone read out the mini-sermon that went along with it, and there you have it...carolizing. Evangelism coupled with caroling. *A novel idea*, I thought. Maybe it would even make me famous one day.

Over the years, I have done "carolizing" with many groups, and it is always a fun and special time. Believers are challenged to share the gospel, not just sing. Listeners get to hear the gospel, not just a familiar Christmas carol. It's always been a win-win.

One particular year of carolizing sticks out in my memory, and it started with our plans not working out. We had gathered a group to go to a local college to do some carolizing. When we arrived at the college, which was about twenty-five minutes away, we were disappointed to find out that the campus had closed early for Christmas, and there was nobody there. I felt a bit embarrassed that I asked all these people (there were about fifteen) to come on out, and never double-checked the dates for Christmas break. It was just one of those things that slipped my mind.

As I was thinking about what to do, one lady said, "Well, why don't we just go to the mall in town and carol outside there?" The idea caught me a bit off guard, but I figured, *Why not!* So we all got into our cars and drove to the mall. The parking lot was packed, and we saw lots of people going in and out.

Our group gathered outside the mall, prayed, and then simply began to sing the carols. They sounded great, but I still wanted to see if there was any chance we could possibly sing inside. "Um, I don't think we can do that," one concerned person said. I told them I was going to go and speak to the mall security and see if we could.

As I walked in, I said the brief prayer that I had grown accustomed to praying in my ministry, "Lord, this is a crazy idea, I have no idea what I'm doing, but I pray for your favor and that You would be glorified, Amen." That has become my most common prayer! I saw a security officer and went up to him.

"Hi, sir, my name is Tim and I am with the Cherry City Carolers, a traveling caroling group. I was wondering if we could do a little Christmas concert in the mall for you all right now?" Now, just to clear my record, the city we come from is nicknamed the Cherry City, and we were caroling, and we did travel to get there, so I figured the name Cherry City Carolers was not technically a lie. I'd like to call it a stretch of reality.

The guard looked at me, puzzled, and said, "Hmm....Do you have an area reserved?"

I told him no, and that our arriving there was a result of a "cancelled previous caroling performance" at a local college. I did not really tell him that the cancelled part was because of my lack of preparation, but figured that was not really too important.

"Well, let's go speak to the mall manager and see what she says."

Before I knew it, I was in the office of the mall manager. I repeated who I was, the "caroling group" I was with, and eagerly awaited her response.

"Well, this is the best thing I have ever heard of! Jason, will you take them to the main stage in the food court area and have them set up? Do you need anything? Can we help in any way?"

I was shocked and did not really know what to say other than, "Um, no, we don't need anything other than maybe make a few announcements over the loudspeaker to tell people where we will be?"

Before I knew it, I was telling the others what had happened, and setting up on the mini bleachers they had, all the while hearing announcements on the overhead speakers: "Attention mall shoppers, in five minutes we will have a special holiday treat from the Cherry City Carolers in our food court area as they will be putting on a Christmas concert."

As we heard that over the loudspeaker, someone said, "Tim, what in the world did you do?! We are not a caroling group! We sound horrible, actually, and we sure don't have a concert!" The overall feeling of the group was a mix of people being excited, and others dreading what was about to take place, and maybe even a bit upset at me for getting us in this situation.

"Well, we are in it now, so let's just have fun, sing our hearts out, and pray as we do." The next thirty minutes were a mix of awkward looks, out-of-tune carols, forgotten lines, and even an occasional laugh. But we sure had fun. During our "concert," I could not help but notice one man who seemed to really be listening to our carols. Most folks would stop for a minute or two, realize we were horrible singers, and move on to their shopping. But this one guy was tuned in. He never took his eyes off us.

As we finished, I went up to him and introduced myself, and asked him what he thought of the "concert." To my utter shock, he loved it and started to ask questions about the meanings of the carols, which led to more questions about God. Thirty minutes later, this man surrendered his life to Jesus right there in the food court, as a result of our lame caroling concert.

I learned that day that when plans get muffed, come up with a new one, because God will work in anything you commit to Him. Oftentimes, we have to step out of our comfort zones to do the things God is calling us to do. I learned that God can literally work through anything, so long as our motive is to give Him glory. I learned that the Lord is after individuals, as much as He is after the masses. Our plans got messed up that day all so that this one man, in a food court in a mall, could hear a really off-key, out-of-tune Christmas concert put on by a bunch of normal people, and through that, step from the kingdom of darkness into the kingdom of light.

Questions to Ponder

1. How intentional are you at taking circumstances and turning them into opportunities for the sharing of the gospel?

2. Why would God choose to work through our own weaknesses and shortcomings?

3. Is there something "out of the box" you can do right now to share the gospel with others?

Civil War Salvation

And whatever you do in word or deed, do all in the name of the Lord Jesus, giving thanks through Him to God the Father. – Colossians 3:17

As I waited for the sound of the fife music to start, I knew this was going to be a staff meeting to go down in the history books. At least, it would in terms of being one of the most awkward. I adjusted my belt, haversack, and rifle, making sure my bayonet was fitted correctly. There I was, dressed up as a Civil War Union soldier, getting ready to give a message on Colossians 3 to our staff at YWAM Salem. I decided it would be a creative way to illustrate Paul's command to the Colossians to put off the old man and put on the new man.

As the fife music began, that was my cue, and I entered through the back of the room and began my march to the front. Immediately I was greeted with lots of laughs, fun-loving comments, weird looks, eye rolls, the shaking of heads, and the whole gamut of emotional responses that made me immediately second-guess whether this was the right idea. People immediately got out their phones to video and take pictures. *Well*, I thought, *I'm in it now, so better just go for it.* I had a fun time sharing the message, and to be truthful, I think the wearing of the outfit thing worked out pretty well, and drove the point home.

As the meeting ended, I went back to my car to get my change of clothes so that I could head to the local college to do some evangelism with our team. There was just one major problem. When I opened my car door, I immediately realized that I forgot my clothes at home! I did not want to waste the time to drive all the way home, change, and drive back. "What are you going to do?" asked one of my friends who was going with us to the college.

"Well, I guess I'm going to the college as a Civil War Soldier." The look on my friend's face told me that either I was crazy, or that he was doing the best he could not to laugh and run away. I still don't know which is true. So we hopped in the van and headed out. I remember praying something like, "Lord, I really feel like an idiot, but please, use this forgetful brain of mine to bring You glory today through this outfit." When I walked on campus, it felt like I was naked. People were staring at me like I just landed from another planet. "Well, I got people's attention; now it's up to you, Lord."

Eventually, a guy approached me and asked me, "I gotta ask, man, what's up with the outfit?" It dawned on me that I never actually thought about how I would talk to people about Jesus using this costume, so I blurted out the first thing that came to my mind. "Thanks for asking. Obviously, you can see that something seems a bit off with me wearing a costume like this in today's society. If you saw a guy dressed up walking around looking like this, you would probably think something's out of whack, correct?"

Without waiting an instant, he responded, "Yep!"

"Well," I responded, "When you look at the world today, do things seem to be as they should, or do things seem to be out of place or off, like my outfit?" And there it was...the beginning of a gospel-centered conversation. All of a sudden, this young man began to share with me his perspective, opinions, and even his life story. He shared about the struggles he was having with his wife, and how he was always bothered about not knowing what happens after a person dies. He laid out his fears. He was being real. It's amazing how open people can be when you show interest in their lives. The costume I had on was no longer the focus of our conversation.

As we continued to talk, I shared the gospel with him, and to my absolute joy and amazement, this young man knelt down on the common green of the college with me and accepted Christ into his life. With desperation, he surrendered to the lordship of the King of Kings.

What I learned that day was that God can use anything to bring people to Him. That day He used a Civil War reenactor's outfit. I learned that sometimes you just have to do crazy-weird things to reach people; sometimes you have to go against the grain of what culture says to reach the lost. I learned that God can use our mistakes. When I forgot to bring my clothes with me, that was a mistake, but God used my mistake for His glory. Amen for that! If God uses our mistakes often for His glory, then He is going to get a lot of glory through me, because I make lots of mistakes.

I also learned that the Lord is always searching for those who are searching for Him. That guy was the only person I spoke to that day. Just one conversation.

He was searching, and God was ready to answer, even if it was in the form of a weird guy in a Civil War costume.

Questions to Ponder

1. Sometimes we doubt God can use us for great things. Are there any areas in which you doubt the Lord can use you for His glory? Why?

2. How comfortable are you at interrupting strangers to talk to them about the gospel, or do you prefer to talk to those you know?

3. How are you attracting others to intentional conversations about Jesus?

Coffee, Donuts, and Evangelism

For the equipping of the saints for the work of service, to the building up of the body of Christ. – Ephesians 4:12

As I picked up the coffee and donuts, I knew it was going to be a great day. Any day that starts with coffee, donuts, and evangelism is starting in the right place as far as I'm concerned. I've never trusted anyone who is opposed to coffee and donuts, but that has nothing to do with this story, so we shall proceed.

The sun was shining as, one by one, pastors began to enter our office for our "Pulpit to Pavement" outreach. This is an outreach we do a few times a year to provide intentional evangelism for pastors in our city. Gather pastors together, take them to do evangelism. Plain and simple. This is truly a special time.

As the pastors slowly began to talk over their coffee and donuts, introducing themselves to each other, there was a light tension in the air. Not a bad tension, but a "What in the world am I doing here?" and "Who are all these people?" type of tension. It was the type of tension you get when you show up to a family reunion or maybe even a homeschool dance...it always starts off a bit weird, and many wonder how they ended up there and when they can leave.

Pastors are by nature a territorial and protective lot, so they were, in a way, seeing who was at the poker table and who was playing what hand. Many of the pastors knew me and our ministry, but there were a bunch that had not yet met us or even heard much about the ministry, but had been invited (if you want pastors to show up to something, offer coffee and donuts and it's usually a shoo-in).

Picture the scene of a typical "Pulpit to Pavement." Slowly, pastors begin to show up to the office. The Baptist pastor comes with his tattered Bible for all to see. (Baptists' Bibles are usually large and black, in case you are wondering.) The Lutheran pastor wonders if it's okay to bring a beer to the shindig. The Pentecostal pastor walks with the energy of someone who has had a bit too much caffeine in the morning, and calls everyone brother or sister. The "non-denominational" pastor feels a bit out of place, like a kid with no one to play with on the playground. The Calvary Chapel pastor shows up late as usual, casual, typically wearing a Hawaiian shirt. Then there is the Assemblies of God pastor, who makes prayer time awkward by constantly saying "Yes, Lord" after every word. And let's not forget the Reformed pastor who usually takes all the fun out of the room by making some comment about proper doctrine. The Presbyterian is always the best-dressed. Maybe you even get a pastor of a "progressive church." He usually has lots of tattoos and smells like some sort of incense, and is sporting a U2 shirt. Yes, "Pulpit to Pavement" is a mixed bag of theological views and traditions...and I love it.

After explaining how the day would go, and doing a little training, we split the pastors up into groups of two and send them out to different street corners. For many of them, it was their first time ever doing evangelism like this, so I knew it would be stretching. Add to that the uncomfortable factor of having them use some of our props like a coffin, limits and comfort zones were being pushed.

As I began to walk around and pray for the pastors, I saw some wonderful things happening. I saw pastors from different churches in the same city, who had never met each other before, getting to know each other. I saw pastors getting time away from "church duties" and being able to just get back to the basics of sharing the gospel. I saw pastors laughing together, praying with each other, and encouraging each other. It was a beautiful thing.

When we returned to the office after a few hours of evangelism, the atmosphere in the room was no longer quiet and awkward, as it had been in the beginning of the day. Now it was vibrant and full of conversation. In two hours' time, these pastors became friends and family in Christ. And it was the sharing of the gospel that brought them together. I saw pastors laying down their denominational differences, and being about the business of preaching Christ crucified. I saw the body of Christ coming together, not for a conference...not for a seminar...not for a training time...but for evangelism. The simple sharing of the gospel. That is the best unifier of the church, and it will always be. I saw pastors encouraged to boldly share Christ, and then encourage those in their churches to do so.

Out of that "Pulpit to Pavement" outreach we have seen many people come and partner with us, and it is such a blessing to work alongside the local churches of our city to share the gospel. The friendships and even partnerships forged out of this outreach have been amazing, and continue to grow. It is truly amazing how the gospel message brings people together, and when you throw donuts and coffee into the equation, it's a grand slam.

Questions to Ponder

1. How familiar are you with the beliefs of other Christian denominations?

2. In what ways does diversity in the body of Christ give the Christian faith credibility?

3. How can you personally rally others around the sharing of the gospel today?

Don't Take the Bait

But refuse foolish and ignorant speculations, knowing that they produce quarrels. – 2 Timothy 2:23

As the two ladies approached me, I could tell it was going to be an interesting conversation. They had just about every form of LGBTQ-affirming indicators you could imagine on their clothes. The rainbow t-shirt, the "Love Has No Gender" slogan on their backpack, and the fact they were holding hands were pretty good indicators as to the type of people I was about to speak with.

Yep, they were on a mission to "have it out" with an evangelical male Christian. I knew this for a few reasons. First, I was standing next to a sign that said, "The Gospel Guy," which is about as blatant and direct a sign as you can get in terms of letting people know who I was, and what I was about. Another indicator was that their body language told me they wanted to fight, not talk. Then, the third, most blatant indicator was when they stopped in front of me, and said, "Hey, Gospel Guy!" And as I looked at them, they gave each other a more-than-affectionate kiss, then turned to me and said, "Do you think this is sin?"

They chuckled and laughed, and I obviously felt very awkward and embarrassed. I also felt sad, as these two were very broken, hurt, and confused individuals. They wanted a fight. Years of ministry has taught me that many people love to get a reaction just for the sake of getting a reaction. I was not going to fall for that. Many people will try to get you to say something, or react in a certain way, simply to justify the reason they hate you as a Christian.

I was not going to take the bait, and I asked them, "What are your names?" They looked at each other in a bit of shock. My response caught them off guard. They obviously were geared up for another Christian to lash out in anger at them, and try to throw a little fire and brimstone at them.

They told me their names, and then I responded to their question. "I tell you what, I will answer your question if you will first tell me what you believe sin to be? Can we do that?"

Still a bit befuddled that I was actually cordially engaging them in conversation, they relaxed a bit, and said, "Sure. I think sin is different for everyone. For you it may be one thing, for me it may mean another. You don't have the right to tell me what sin is, and I don't have the right to tell you what sin is." They continued their extended explanation, which was just another form of them justifying the lifestyle they chose and their rejection of God, but I continued to listen until they asked me a question. "So, you heard what we think, but what are your thoughts, do you think homosexuality is a sin?"

I then went on to explain the difference between subjective and objective truth. I went into a few different illustrations about what the Bible says about sin. I could tell I had their attention, and that they were truly pondering what I was saying. As our conversation, which had now turned into about forty-five minutes, came to a close, I said to them, "Can I ask you one final question?" They nodded their heads.

"Do you see where I'm coming from here? The difference between you and me is not what we believe about sin, but what we believe about God. If we throw God out, sin is irrelevant, because it would not exist outside of a God. We need someone to define for us what sin is, and as I have laid out in my case, that person to me is Jesus. Jesus defines my morality. I don't get to define morality." I continued to press them a bit. "Now, if you're being honest, would you admit that one of the big reasons you don't want anything to do with this Jesus guy is because you both don't want anyone defining morality for you, but you would rather define morality on your own?"

They both gave a reflective look, and answered, "I guess that's exactly what we are saying." I replied, "So can you see now why I believe your lifestyle is sinful? It's not me hating you, it's me submitting to a higher moral authority in my life and getting my definition of sin from Him, not myself or others."

They both nodded, and one of them said, "You know, that makes sense, I guess, if I'm coming from your side. I've never heard it put that way before. Usually, Christians just tell me how I'm a sinner and God hates gay people. I appreciate how you described why you believe what you do, and thanks for not chewing us out." They politely said goodbye.

As they walked away, I pondered our conversation. I learned that so many people are misunderstood, and how having a simple conversation with them can break down barriers. I learned how key it is in witnessing to not take the bait others may intentionally set before you. When we are good listeners, people naturally want to open up with us and be real.

I learned that, sadly, people will reject the One who loves them the most simply because they want to be god of their lives. The Scriptures are true, and in the end many will choose sin over salvation, and this breaks the heart of God. I learned that you can have great discussions over volatile issues of the day with people, when you actually do what the Bible says to do: be kind, compassionate, listen, avoid arguing, and so on. Lastly, I learned that oftentimes, you may be "lumped" together with a group of people who have caused harm to others, and what a great opportunity it is to shatter that stereotype when you share the love and truth of Christ with people in sincerity and compassion.

Questions to Ponder

1. Do you hold a conversation, rather than arguing a point, in evangelism?

2. Why is it so important, as an ambassador of Christ, to know how to respond to people in different ways?

3. How can you break down misconceptions about Christianity with others?

Don't Worry About it, I'll Take Care of It

Serving the Lord with all humility... – Acts 20:19

I pulled up to our office one morning and saw the stuff that was lying on the pavement outside the office door. I began to grumble and complain inside. *Aw, man, not again, for crying out loud!* I thought. I could see the trail of McDonald's french-fry containers, napkins, crushed potato chips, plastic forks, and the usual stuff that often gets left behind by a homeless person after they have slept under the awning of our office to stay out of the rain. Thankfully, there did not appear to be any needles this time, but then again, I was still in my car so I had no idea what was actually awaiting me.

A few years ago, we never had this problem of people sleeping in front of our office, but over the past few years it had become a big problem—not just in front of our office, but in front of many offices in our area. It got to the point where local businesses had to get a city ordinance and post signs that said "No Trespassing" in front of our windows to keep people from not just sleeping in front of our office, but also using the space to drink, do drugs, and all the other terrible things that the world offers and destroys people's lives. I guess this also ensured some sort of legal structure to hold accountable the people who did not seem to care if you asked them to leave your office area.

I did not realize the magnitude of the issue until one morning, I pulled up early and saw George, the cobbler, cleaning up a huge mess in front of my office. "George, let me take care of that. I'm so sorry about this. When did this happen?"

George replied, "Oh, I have been cleaning up like this in front of your office for weeks now in the morning." I had no idea that each morning George had to deal with this mess. So, I apologized and told him I would take care of it. Of course, this meant me actually putting up the "No Trespassing" sign. We were the last office on our block to put up a "no trespassing" sign. It was sort of a "Custer's Last Stand" of compassion...now even that was gone. It just seems tough to tell people with no homes they can't sleep under something that keeps them dry. But I knew I had to, it was the right thing to do for our neighbors, and George did not deserve to have to deal with that type of stuff.

I got out of my van and as I approached my office door, I was greeted by the terrible smell of urine and poop. Right in front of our office, on the sidewalk and all over our windows, was the source of the terrible smells. Whoever slept there that night had decided to use our windows and sidewalk as their bathroom, and it was nasty. Covering my nose and taking a deep breath, I leapfrogged over all the stuff and stepped into our office. Inside was my friend Shane, and Larry, one of our interns who just happened to be with us for his second day of his evangelism internship. They were talking and I said, "Have you guys seen outside?"

They looked at me and said yes, and for a moment there was silence. "I'm gonna call the city to see if they can send a crew to clean it up." Without even waiting for them to say anything, I stepped outside the office, frustrated, irritated, and fed up. After being on hold for what seemed like forever, I finally was able to speak to someone who very clearly told me that it was not the responsibility of the city to clean it up but, since I am the "business owner," the responsibility fell to me.

"I don't think you understand what I'm talking about here," I said. "This stuff is gonna need some serious power hosing and some disinfectant to take care of it all. Not to mention, much of it is on the sidewalk in front of my office, which is city property." My plea for compassion and understanding went unheard as the lady told me once again it was my responsibility. Like a toddler stomping their feet when told they had to wait until supper for food, I returned to the office and said, "Well, the city said they are not going to do anything about it, and we need to clean it up. What are we gonna do?" The last thing we wanted to do at that time was clean up that type of stuff. I was trying to think how in the world we were going to tackle the issue. The only thing we had in our office was some paper towels and hand sanitizer!

"Hey, guys, you two head out and do evangelism, I'll take care of it. I'll clean it up." Larry's words stopped me in my tracks.

"What? Larry, this is your second day with us, I can't ask you to clean that up, that's ridiculous."

His response was sobering, "You didn't ask me to clean it up, I WANT to clean it up. Now go tell people about Jesus, and I'll take care of this. I have some stuff at my house I'll run and grab, and I'll clean it up." And that was that. I've heard hundreds of sermons about being a servant, and taking the low position of humility, and all of them combined together did not impact me as much as what Larry said, and then did. I was humbled. Here was a guy who should have gone out to do evangelism; after all, it was part of the internship he paid for, and yet he humbled himself, took the lowly way, and taught me so much about preferring others, and what it means to be a servant.

So he cleaned it up. It took him the rest of the morning to do so, and when I returned after doing evangelism you could not even tell the stuff had been there. He used to be a bus driver in the city, and I would always refer to him as "Larry the Bus Driver." After that day, I think I'll refer to him now as "Larry the Plumber."

I learned that day how humility really looks. I learned putting feet to what the Bible teaches is hard, but when it is done, it is powerful. Larry showed me what it meant to wash the feet of others that day. Larry finished our internship and then joined our team full-time, and through his example teaches me and others so much about loving people, and being a servant.

Questions to Ponder

1. How does being a servant relate to evangelism?

2. Check your heart: are there things in life that you think you are "too good" to do?

3. How does being great in the eyes of God differ from being great in the eyes of the world?

Evangelism Means Fellowship

*Behold, how good and how pleasant it is for brothers
to dwell together in unity! – Psalm 133:1*

I was at a Starbucks doing some work one day when I
got a phone call from a random guy named Nate. "Hi,
I was listening to your podcast and am really interested
in your ministry. I've been wanting to become more
effective and intentional with my evangelism, so I
wanted to give you a call and hear more about your
ministry." At first, I was surprised to find out anyone
even listened to our podcast, so I knew this was going
to be a special day!

As I sipped my coffee, I spent the next thirty minutes or
so talking to Nate about our ministry, and in particular
the evangelism internship we offer. "Sign me up!" Nate
said. The next week, Nate began his internship and
started to grow in his witness in many ways. But there
was something I noticed about Nate that was a bit
different from many of the interns who came through
our program. Most interns want to have just a small
briefing time when they arrive and then head out to do
evangelism straight away. Nate seemed to really enjoy
the time of fellowship before we headed out, and did
not seem too bothered if the evangelism time was cut
short, so long as he was having fellowship with us.

As the weeks went on, one morning during our typical
briefing time before we headed out, Nate asked if he

could share a little bit about something he was going through. "Of course!" I said. Nate then went on to share some personal things he was presently going through, and then at the end, he said something that really was an eye-opener to me. "You know, I have been going to church for years, but I have never felt like I could ever find like-minded people who took sharing the gospel seriously like you guys. I have always been afraid to keep bringing it up, because honestly, I get shut down a lot. You guys are the only people I feel comfortable sharing this stuff with." Then Nate began to cry.

Now, Nate is a prison guard by profession, so he's not your cry-on-a-whim, sappy type of guy. He truly meant what he said, and he was very emotional about it. "You know, I reached out to this ministry because I wanted to grow in evangelism, which I am. But I think the bigger blessing, and actually the reason the Lord had me do this, is because I needed this type of fellowship I was not getting elsewhere. You guys have become like family to me, and for that I am so grateful."

It was a powerful moment. And from that point on, this little ministry became like church for Nate. He went on to finish his internship and now volunteers a day a week with the ministry. His stories of how the internship has helped his witness in the prisons are very encouraging as well.

Many times, God uses our interests to perform a different work in our life we may not have been expecting. Nate thought the internship was going to help him become more effective in evangelism, and it did, but it also brought him the fellowship he desperately needed. Evangelism created fellowship for Nate. I learned that just because people go to church, that does not mean they are receiving all they need. For whatever reason, Nate was not able to find like-minded people at church when it came to evangelism, and when he found that in our ministry, it was life-giving for him.

Church definitely is not a building, and can happen anywhere, at any time. We are the body of Christ, and when we look at the Christian life as being a part of that body, church is something we do, not go to. I learned that sincerity and vulnerability is a powerful platform for deep relationships. Nate was very humble and open with us about his life and his struggles, and that takes guts to do. But when he did that, it allowed us to begin a whole new level of friendship with Nate that we cherish to this day. I was reminded how the proclamation of the gospel always provides opportunity to get to know others in the body of Christ, and it will always be the rally point of our lives.

Questions to Ponder

1. Would you consider yourself a sincere and vulnerable person with others?

2. Why is it important to have a good group of fellow believers to walk through life with?

3. How are you actively involving others into your life today?

Eye-Opener

*But because of the Pharisees they were not confessing
Him, lest they should be put out of the synagogue. –
John 12:42*

It had been a long morning doing our Crosswalk
outreach, where we drag a cross through our city in
silence. Only a few more people from the group were
left to drag the cross, so I handed it to the next person,
a young high school student named Lizzy. She picked
up the cross and began to drag it down the sidewalk.

I have dragged the cross many times, and have run this
outreach many times, so I know what to expect. It is
generally a very solemn, quiet, reflective time. But
today was going to be a day I would never forget,
when something very unexpected happened.

As Lizzy continued to drag the cross, a group of about
five people approached us from the other direction. As
they came closer to us, one of the people in the group
said, "Lizzy, is that you?" "Oh my goodness, it is you!
What are you doing?" It was an awkward moment as
Lizzy stopped in her tracks, her face became red, and
she realized that right before her eyes was a group of
kids that she knew from her school.

She tried her best to act normal, but you could tell it
was a difficult moment for her. "Well, I'm on a mission
trip and I'm dragging this cross around town, and I'm

doing it to reflect on what Jesus did for me and the world." Lizzy just repeated our standard response we suggest to people if asked that question, and you could tell from how she said it, it was robotic.

Then, something profound and revealing happened as her friends responded. "Oh, that's cool, I guess. I never even knew you went to church or were a Christian." And with that they passed by and headed the other direction. Now, we were in the center of the city, and cars were driving here and there, the noises of a city were all around us, yet it seemed as if you could have heard a pin drop at that moment. Lizzy stood there, and she began to cry.

"Are you okay, Lizzy?" I asked. Her leader came up and asked her the same question, and finally after what felt like an eternity of crying, Lizzy said, "I am so ashamed. I feel terrible. Here I am dragging a cross and kids from my school don't even know I'm a Christian." It was a painful but beautiful moment. "I have been such a fake. My faith is so superficial, and I realized that just now. Today is an eye-opener for me." Her youth pastor began to walk alongside her and encourage her.

I learned that day that we all can fake our faith really easily, but God has a way of revealing the depth—or as in Lizzy's case, the shallowness—of it. He does this for our own good, not to shame us but to reveal our heart's attitude. I learned that the cross will always be a fork in the road for people. It took a literal wooden cross to get Lizzy to see where her faith needed some reflection. The cross is something we are to bring with us wherever we go, not just on a mission trip. I learned that as Christians we often want the rewards of what

Jesus has done for us, but we really do not want the cost that may come with following Him. Lizzy learned that day that it is easy to believe in Jesus, but to confess Him before others is a lot harder.

Questions to Ponder

1. Are you "hiding" your faith in any way from others? Why?

2. What "cross" may the Lord be putting in your life today?

3. What is the value of a faith that believes, but does not confess?

From Judge to Father

He got up and came to his father. But while he was still a long way off, his father saw him and felt compassion for him, and ran and embraced him, and kissed him. – Luke 15:20

Every now and then I meet someone who is so zealous for evangelism, I wonder if even John the Baptist would envy them. You know the type: the person who has such an eternal concern for everyone, they cannot help but share the gospel with others, friends or strangers. It is who they are, how they live, and how they think.

Brandon is one of those guys. He eats, drinks, breathes, and lives evangelism. His passion to see people come to know Jesus is admirable, and if I only had a quarter of his passion I would say I'm doing alright! Brandon decided to do the evangelism internship we offer because he wanted to be better equipped in his role as an evangelist in his local church. I was humbled when he asked to be a part, as I knew he was a qualified, well-equipped guy already.

From the get-go, Brandon was like a Brahma bull let out of the chute at a rodeo. And in his case, unfortunately, there were a lot of clowns out there he could not wait to gore with his horns. His evangelism style resembled that of a fast-paced comet. Intense. To the point. Direct. Even abrasive at times. He liked to be right and loved the challenge of an argument. Clearly, we could teach this guy nothing about being zealous for souls! Brandon was teachable, and took our critiques and counsel with humility. As the internship went on, I began to see a change in this young man's witnessing style. He became better at listening, better at asking questions, better about talking with people, not just at them. But Brandon, like all of us, had an Achilles heel to his witnessing style. Brandon was bent on introducing people to God the Judge.

As the weeks went by during his internship, I could see he was getting stressed and tired. He grew frustrated with the people he was speaking to, which happens to us all, but something deep inside Brandon was causing a little bit more stress and tension than was necessary. After he showed me a list of goals he had made for the year, I realized that this guy had way too much on his plate, and he was putting demands upon himself that were just too much.

We went out for coffee one afternoon. As we talked, Brandon began to open up, and before long, I began to see where the frustration he was having was coming from. In the sincere goodness of his heart to please God, Brandon was operating out of a works-based mentality, constantly trying to prove to God his worth and value. He so badly wanted approval from others, he had forgotten that the one he needed approval from the most already gave him all the approval he needed when He died on the cross. I looked at Brandon and asked him if I could be blunt with him. "I wouldn't have it any other way," he said.

"Brandon, I love you, man, but I fear you only relate to God as your Judge, not as your Father. Do you understand the difference and what I'm getting at?" To this day I remember the look on his face, as if he heard something that he had never heard before in that simple statement.

With tears in his eyes he said, "You are absolutely right, Tim, you hit the nail on the head." I could tell the Lord had brought up something of extreme importance to Brandon, the type of thing that would be a "game changer" for him and the way he did evangelism from that point on. We talked for a while after that and it was one of the sweetest times of ministry I have ever had: one brother to another, being there for each other. Brandon's style of evangelism was never the same after that. Sure, he is still direct, blunt, and to the point—that is just who he is. But he now brings God the Judge and God the Father into his evangelism, and it is a beautiful thing to see.

I learned so much from Brandon that day. We all have areas we need to work on. Being honest in our weaknesses is key to becoming more like Jesus. God will always use our rough edges to ultimately bring Him glory. I learned that when we are open to advice and counsel, we are soft, moldable clay that the Lord can use. Brandon is a great example of how the Lord can shape our understanding of His amazing character, and allow that balanced understanding to form our evangelistic witness. Brandon is a great friend to this day, and is one of our mentors in our evangelism internship. It is a joy to see him help people grow in their evangelism, and be able to use his journey to help people refine their "rough edges." By the way, did I mention we all have them?

Questions to Ponder

1. How open are you to the advice and counsel of other people?

2. How do you properly articulate the whole character of God in your witnessing?

3. Would you say you lean more on the law side or the grace side of the gospel? What can you do to become more balanced?

I Thought You Two Were Loony

We are fools for Christ's sake. – 1 Corinthians 4:10

"I actually stopped and talked to you guys because I wanted to see who in the world would be crazy enough to stand in this type of weather all day long talking to strangers. I gotta be honest, I came with the mindset that you guys may be a bit off your rocker."

These words came from a guy who would later become a great friend of ours, and a partner in ministry. It was a cold winter morning as my friend Ryan and I stood outside in front of the mall doing evangelism. It happened to be one of those days that was bone-chillingly cold, and the rain seemed to be falling from the ground up, it was so wet out. There is no such thing as "fair weather" evangelists in the Northwest. We often chuckle when people ask us, "How do you evangelism in the rain?" I'm not sure if they really know what they are asking. It would be like asking a person in Alaska, "How do you do evangelism in the snow? Or asking a person in Mexico, "How do you do evangelism when it's hot out?" Our response to that funny question is simply, "We do evangelism in the rain." Anyway, on to the story.

On that morning, Ryan and I had sat in our office watching the rain pour down and listening to the brisk wind. Both of us were thinking it was going to be a miserable, cold morning. On a day like that, we were pretty sure not many people were going to be out anyway. I recall saying, "Maybe we should just stay in and pray." That's code for "I really don't want to do evangelism in this type of weather."

It is quite humorous, and maybe a bit sad, how quickly prayer times can be a safe excuse for not doing evangelism. But I've been guilty of that a time or two. After both of us realized that we were being "fair weather evangelists," and both felt a little built guilty, we decided to head out. As we grabbed coffee on the way Ryan and I made fun of each other, trying the best we could to outdo the other with "loving insults" towards each other. Ryan and I have always prided ourselves in this regard, and it is something we take very seriously. Humor is something that often gets overlooked in evangelism; but when Ryan and I get together, we often have no problem focusing on the humor, but overlook evangelism! All joking aside, though, Ryan is the type of guy I'd storm the gates of hell with. He's a great friend, a funny guy, and a gifted, tenacious evangelist.

The morning played out to be a rough one, and nobody seemed eager to talk, until this guy walked up to us and said, "Hi, my name is Craig, and I'm a pastor in town. I just have to ask: What's your deal, and who are you guys?" Thus began a great discussion which led to him telling us that he was a pastor in our city and had seen us on multiple occasions, always wondering who we were and what we were about. For some reason this was the day he decided to talk to us.

After we explained the nuts and bolts about ourselves and our ministry, his face relaxed a bit, he took a deep breath, and said, "Wow, praise God. So you guys are just normal people, talking to people about Jesus! For a while now, I honestly thought you guys may be a bit loony." And that started a fantastic friendship.

The next week we went out for coffee and got to know Craig better. He even invited me to preach in his church, and was eager to see how he could plug the people from his church into our ministry. To this day, Craig remains a dear friend and mentor. Not only did he begin to come out and do evangelism with us, he also is now one of our mentors for our Face to Face evangelism internship we offer here in our city.

We often make assumptions that can put up walls rather than build bridges. Craig made an "assumption" about the "type" of people we were, but when he realized we were just the opposite, great things began to happen. I assumed Craig may be just "another" pastor who would be all talk, no action when, it came to getting his church involved in our evangelism. We all run the risk of unfair assumptions.

Thank the Lord, both Craig and I had our assumptions shattered. I learned that pastors are hungry for people who have different gifts, and they desire those gifts be used for the people of their churches. I was so encouraged when Craig saw in our ministry something his church not only could plug into, but desperately needed. I learned that oftentimes, some of the coolest works of God begin with curiosity. Craig's curiosity led to a great friendship and partnership in ministry. Our curiosity in his interest led to him appreciating the time we took to hear his heart for his church. I learned that we all need to get to know people, even if they may be people we think we may not want to get to know. That's exactly what Jesus did. He came to know people whom He knew would reject him. So must we.

Questions to Ponder

1. How have you found yourself making false assumptions about others?

2. In what ways does making assumptions affect your desire to share the gospel?

3. When people observe you and your actions, do you think you represent Christ well?

I'm Praying For You

And the Lord opened the servant's eyes, and he saw;
and behold, the mountain was full of horses and
chariots of fire all around Elisha. – 2 Kings 6:17

Many times, I think back to the beginning of our ministry here in Salem. In 2013 I decided to take a few mornings a week and go do evangelism by myself. Often it was hard, lonely, and many times simply discouraging. Slowly, over time, others began to join with me and that helped tremendously, but it was still difficult. I guess that comes with the territory of bringing the gospel to a lost world.

One afternoon I was standing on a corner, just observing the people of our city. When you spend enough time somewhere, you begin to see familiar people. The businessman always walking to a meeting, the mom with the stroller and her Starbucks coffee, the homeless guy with a cardboard sign, the security guy taking a smoke break, were all familiar sights.

Another familiar sight was watching the city workers who were responsible for checking parking meters and ticketing cars. I've always felt badly for these guys since, rain or shine, hot or cold, they had to walk miles and miles a day checking on meters. Often I would see them writing a ticket only to have some angry person come out of a store and start chewing them out. Talk about a lose-lose situation.

Anyway, I used to see these guys all the time, but had never actually engaged them in conversation. On this particular day I was feeling a bit discouraged after spending a morning getting rejected by people, and not having very many conversations, when one of the city workers walked up to me and said, "Hi, my name is Tim, and I'm a Christian. I just wanted you to know that I see you guys out here all the time, and I pray for you all day long as I'm walking my route checking meters. So, consider me your prayer covering while you're out here."

We then began to talk, sharing our stories, and it led to him asking me to pray for him as he witnessed to his coworkers. He asked me if I would begin to pray for him as he wanted to get a job as a camp director, but there were many things that needed to fall into place. He was grateful for the job he had, but it was by no means where he wanted to spend the rest of his days. He shared about how lost many people were in his line of work.

When Tim walked away from our first meeting, I was rejuvenated to share the gospel. There was something special about knowing that there was a guy praying for us all the time. I also felt honored to be able to pray for him and his witness to his coworkers. I recall so many times we would be in an intense witnessing time, and I would see Tim walk by us and simply give us that look that said, "I've got you guys. I'm praying for you." Sometimes, he would even stop near us and pretend like he was reading a meter, and I could tell he was just listening to our conversation. I knew why. He was praying for us in those conversations, and taking the battle into the heavenlies on our behalf.

That first conversation started a great friendship. Tim approached me one day with a big smile on his face. He told me that the Lord had answered his prayers for that camp job, and that in a few weeks he would be quitting his job with the city and going into full-time ministry. I told him I was happy for him, but reminded him that he was already in full-time ministry. "Tim, you've been in full-time ministry since the day I met you and you told us you were interceding for us." He understood what I was trying to get across.

As he walked away, I had mixed emotions. I was so happy for Tim and the new chapter in life he would be entering, but I was also sad that this prayer warrior, who had battled so many times for our evangelism on the streets through his prayers, was no longer going to be a familiar sight. Sure, I knew he would continue to pray for us, but his physical presence would be gone.

I learned a lot from Tim. Our prayers matter, and knowing that there are others in the fight with you is so encouraging and important. Many times I felt alone but there were others, like Tim, with me, and the Lord showed me that we truly are never alone. I learned that you can be an active part in someone's ministry, even if you do not even work with them in ministry. Tim was actively praying for us, and I know that his prayers impacted the growth and effectiveness of our ministry in so many ways.

Tim remains a good friend to this day, and has allowed me and my sons to play airsoft out at the camp he works at a number of times. Each time I step onto the camp where he works, I intentionally lift him up in prayer and go to battle for him in the heavenlies, as he did so many times for me.

Questions to Ponder

1. When you feel alone in ministry, what promises of God can you rely on?

2. Does interceding in prayer for others have a place in your life at this time?

3. How does consistency in prayer relate to your personal evangelism?

Keep That Stuff in the Churches

For we cannot stop speaking what we have seen and heard. – Acts 4:20

It was summertime, which meant we were busy week after week taking high school students out to do evangelism through our Mission Adventures program. Every week, we would receive youth groups from all over the place. They would spend five days with us, and we would train and equip them for evangelism. The weeks were always full, packed with energy and evangelism.

One of the days of the week was spent doing evangelism on our city buses. This was always a stretch for all the students, not to mention us. As I sat down on the bus with the students who were with me, I knew that I needed to go first. One of the perks of being a leader, I guess, is you get to do crazy things like that first, and hope it all works out and that others will follow!

Anyway, I stood up on a pretty full bus and began a simple gospel message. About midway through my message, a lady sitting a few seats away yelled, "Sit down! We don't want to hear any of this stuff." I pretended that I did not even hear her, and continued. She yelled louder. "Shut up and sit down, nobody is listening to you!"

I looked at her and politely said, "Miss, I'm sorry if you do not like what I have to say, but if you would be so kind as to let me finish, I'm almost done." I'm not sure why that set her off, but she stood up and walked right up to me. People were staring at us, and the bus was silent. I could tell the driver felt caught in an uncomfortable situation, which was unfortunate. Every time I rode on the buses I would ask the drivers if I could share a few words, and most of the time they were fine with it, as was this particular driver.

As the lady looked into my eyes, I could see her eyes were filled with hate and rage. She scowled at me as if I had just stolen something from her. The situation was awkward, uncomfortable, and even a bit scary. Her fists were clenched, which made me wonder if I was going to get a "souvenir" from the day. I had no idea what to do, so I just looked away from her and continued with my message.

She yelled louder, right in my face, and then she said something that I'll never forget. With all the force she could muster, she jabbed her finger right into my chest three times, looked me in the eye and yelled, "You keep this stuff in the churches. It's not meant for anywhere but churches, so sit down and shut up!"

"Keep this stuff in the churches!" she said again. When she said that I felt a cold chill go down my spine, and it was at that moment that I knew this was something more than just a lady yelling at me for preaching on a bus. This was the spirit of the age speaking against the proclamation of the gospel. It was the exact thing Satan would say. *Keep the message in the church. Don't bring it to the lost.*

As she began to yell louder, I felt a peace come over me that truly is something hard to explain. Sure, it was an uncomfortable situation, but all the fear left me, and the louder she got, the more I wanted to share the gospel. I had never felt the tangible presence of the Holy Spirit in my life as much as I did those few moments. I did not want the bus driver to have to deal with the situation, so I felt it best to just sit down.

When the bus finished its typical loop route around the city, we got off at the bus station and walked back to our office for a time of debrief with the other groups that went out on other buses. I was excited to share. We all sat down in the office, and I asked, "Would anybody like to share about their time on the buses?"

A few people spoke up, and just as I was about to share what had happened to me, my friend Ryan spoke up. "I'd like to share something, if I may." He began his story. "I stood up on the bus and began to share the gospel. As I was sharing, a man stood up and began to yell at me. I tried to ignore him, but then he got right in my face, and shoved his finger in my chest and said, "You keep this stuff in the church man. Keep it in the churches!"

Everyone that was part of my group on the bus immediately looked at me with shock and amazement as Ryan spoke. I had a tingly chill go down my spine as Ryan continued. "He then kept saying to me to keep it in the churches. Others on the bus began to agree with him, and tell me to shut up, sit down, and keep this stuff I was saying in the churches." Ryan ended by sharing about how it was one of the saddest times of witnessing he had ever had, but at the same time he shared how the peace of God was all over him, and he had no fear. As a matter of fact, it just emboldened him to share the gospel all the more!

I threw my arms in the air and interrupted Ryan. "You have to be kidding me! Did you speak to someone from my group?"

"No," Ryan replied. "Why?"

I then went on to explain what had happened to me. Everyone was amazed: two guys, two different buses, two very similar situations. Almost to the detail, we had not only the same thing happen to us, but we also had the exact same eerie thing said to us: "Keep that stuff in the churches."

We talked about the hate and anger in the people's faces when they said that, and we all knew that it was a demonic spirit out there that day trying to hinder the proclamation of the gospel. We then spent a sweet, rich time in prayer for the people we had encountered that day.

I learned that day that opposition will come in many forms when you share the gospel, whether it comes in the form of simple fear, or the harsh words of others. I learned that demonic forces are very real, and many times can be seen and felt very tangibly. I learned that oftentimes, the peace of God is felt most powerfully in scary, uncertain situations. His peace is felt most tangibly not in the green fields of rest, but in the harsh stormy seas. I learned that there are always others with us in the fight. Ryan and I, though on different buses, were fighting the same battle. Lastly, I learned that one of Satan's main strategies to hinder the spreading of the gospel is to convince Christians that the only place the gospel should be shared is in the church. May we never buy into that lie.

Questions to Ponder

1. How much do you allow fear of man to inhibit your sharing of the gospel with others?

2. How should knowing that the Holy Spirit is not only with us, but also within us, impact our attitudes toward evangelism?

3. In what ways can you encourage and challenge yourself, and your church, to bring the gospel outside of the four walls of your church?

Knock, Knock

And I say to you, ask, and it shall be given to you;
seek, and you shall find; knock, and it shall be opened
to you. – Luke 11:9

I have to be honest, it was a rather "sketchy" neighborhood, and I was not too excited to be knocking on doors, especially when it seemed that every house had blankets kept over the windows by duct tape, and there was a massive pitbull behind every fence or in every house we had been to that morning.

We were out doing "door-to-door" prayer, in which we knock on people's doors, introduce ourselves, and ask them if they need prayer for anything. This is kind of the covert way of doing door-to-door evangelism. I'm not sure why we call it door-to-door prayer, because we always end up sharing the gospel anyway. Personally, I have never really been a fan of door-to-door anything, so this always is a stretch for me, but I knew it would be a huge step of faith for the group of high school students we were leading on outreach that day.

As we went from door to door, we had a good mix of closed doors, no-thank-you's, and an occasional person accepting our request, sharing their needs with us and allowing us to pray for them. We would then try to share the gospel with them, which was always a cool thing to do. Toward the end of our morning we decided to knock on one last door. It took everything within me to approach that door, as I was a bit cynical and thought to myself, *Here we go again, another home where no one answers.*

To my surprise, a young guy named Horatio answered the door. I explained who we were, what we were doing, and asked if we could pray for any needs he might have. He awkwardly looked over his shoulder in his house, pulled the door shut, and stepped out onto the patio where we were standing. He had a surprised look on his face. "You know, this is so weird; I have actually been thinking a lot about God recently."

We talked for the next twenty minutes or so and I could see that he was really open to the gospel. "Horatio, can I ask you a really personal question?"

"Sure," he replied.

"If you died today, and stood before God, do you think He would accept you into heaven?"

"Wow, I've never been asked that before, and I honestly do not know." I took the opportunity to share with him the gospel, and right there on his patio, he surrendered his life to Jesus. I could not believe it. This was the first time in my life this happened in a door-to-door setting. I wish I could say that happened all the time, but in my experience of going door-to-door, it rarely did. I cannot tell you how many hundreds of doors we had knocked on before something like this happened.

In a way, going door-to-door presents you with a real life picture of man's response to the gospel. Many are not interested, many are simply closed, locked, and not willing to even talk, and others, like Horatio, open their lives to the Lord.

As we walked away, the high schoolers with me were enthusiastic. "That was awesome! Can I knock on the next door?" They were motivated by what had just happened.

"Sure," I said. "But to be honest with you, that rarely happens, in my experience." And true to the trend, the next hour was spent knocking on doors that would not open, and of the ones that did open, many simply refused the offer of prayer.

I learned that day that sometimes, you just have to try "one more time" when reaching out to people, because you never know which hearts and minds the Lord has opened. Interrupting people's lives, even if it may be awkward, is worth it if you truly believe the gospel to be what it is: the only hope we have. I learned that God uses closed doors to prepare us for the ones that will open. If every time I did evangelism it was all unicorns and rainbows, I'm not sure what I would do when the floor fell out and rejection was the norm. Evangelism is full of closed doors, but there will always be open ones.

I learned that we often get set in our ways of witnessing, and it is good to be taken out of our comfort zones. I never liked door-to-door stuff, and it is still not my favorite way to witness! But that does not mean it's not good for me to do every now and then. I learned that sometimes, we are the answers to people's prayers and questions. Horatio had been praying and thinking about God, searching for answers, and it just so happened that the Lord allowed us to be part of that answer.

Questions to Ponder:

1. What are the closed doors that discourage you from sharing the gospel with others?

2. Are there any "doors" you need to knock on today?

3. In what ways can you step out of your comfort zone to share the gospel with others today?

Lord, Give Us a Suit

Ask, and it shall be given to you; seek, and you shall find; knock, and it shall be opened to you. – Matthew 7:7

"Lord, give us a suit!" That was a prayer that I had been praying for a few months each morning when we would gather to pray before heading out to do evangelism. What I meant in that prayer was for the Lord to lead a businessman to Him through our evangelism. You know, the nice, clean-cut, well-dressed type that appears to have it all together on the outside.

I'm not a big fan of labeling or broad-stroking people with a general paintbrush of assumptions, but in my years of doing outreach, it seemed that the people in business suits were the hardest to reach. They often just brush by you, flat out ignore you, or appear to be busy, on their way to an appointment perhaps. And maybe many of them are too busy. I sure do not want to judge anyone by their appearance, but I think you can make a good judgment based upon years of the same thing repeating itself.

It also is an interesting observation that many times when I attempted to stop the "suits," the response I would often get was a cordial, polite, "No thanks, I'm good." Talk about a lie from the enemy right there. So many people walk around thinking they are "good," and that applied to most of my experiences doing evangelism in our city to anyone wearing a business suit. So I began to pray for a "suit."

After a few months of praying this, one morning I just felt a very heavy burden to pray for the Lord to send us a "suit." When I began to pray, all I could think of was a person in a suit coming to Jesus. So that's how I prayed, and that's how all the guys who were with me prayed. We sincerely asked God for a "suit" that morning. We then headed out and began to walk to our usual corners where we do outreach.

To be honest, it took me a whole thirty seconds to forget what we had been praying for. I took one of our staff named Luis with me and we went to a common corner in our city, and began to do evangelism. Wouldn't you know it, but the first person who approached us was one of the best-dressed men I have ever seen. He looked like he was on the way to make some multi-million dollar deal with an oil company. He was literally that dressed up. He had headphones on, so I was not expecting him to pay us any attention at all. But, hey, you've got to try.

So I motioned to him and asked him if he had a minute for a conversation. To my shock, he stopped, thought a second or two, and said, "Sure, I have a few minutes. What's up?"

It happened to be close to Christmas, so I told him we were Christians asking people in our city if they celebrated Christmas and what they understood Christmas to be. He told us that he celebrated the holiday, but it had no religious significance whatsoever. As a matter of fact, when I asked him if he knew the Christian story of why we celebrate Christmas, he had no idea.

I then went on to explain to him the true meaning of Christmas, that God came to us in Christ Jesus to save us from our sins and reconcile us back to Him. As he listened, he stopped me and said, "This is so interesting; how did you know this is what I have been thinking about lately? I have been on a personal quest to know more about God, and I have been searching for answers to some of these things."

He then went on to share his personal story, how religion was never really a part of his life, but recently he had begun to think a lot about God, the meaning of life, and so on. We ended up having an amazing thirty-minute discussion, which then led to a great conversation over coffee the following week, which I know will lead to more great conversations as Chris continues to search for truth.

As our conversation ended and Chris walked away, it never even occurred to me what had just happened until Luis looked at me with a big smile on his face and said, "There's our suit!" He was right. Unbelievable. God sent us a "suit" that morning. He sent us literally what we asked for. Not only did he send us a "suit," but he sent us a "suit" who was searching eagerly for something only Jesus can give Him.

On that brisk December day I learned that sometimes God gives us the specific things we pray for. I was reminded to pray specifically, pray with detail, and pray with intention. I was also reminded that we have an amazing God who loves to put all the chess pieces on the board the way He desires. He is constantly connecting our prayers with people who are searching for truth.

Lastly, I was reminded of my lack of faith for the Lord to answer the prayers we pray. After praying for so long for a suit, in many ways I had given up on the Lord answering them. He reminded me that He is a faithful God who always hears our prayers, and who always answers them in His timing and according to His will and purposes.

Questions to Ponder

1. When it comes to praying for people, how specific are you in your prayers?

2. How confident are you that the Lord will not only hear your prayers, but in His ways and timing answer them?

3. How much of your prayer life is focused on praying for the salvation of people?

Man Overboard

Thus Noah did; according to all that God had commanded him, so he did. – Genesis 6:22

No, that can't be a good idea, I thought to myself as I drove down the interstate after a morning of evangelism on a local college campus. *But then again, maybe it is a good idea.*

This has often become the way the Lord leads me to do things. He will plant an idea in my head, and I will try to dismiss the thought as it usually is something that I know is going to stretch me in many ways. Then, over the next few days or weeks, I just can't seem to get the idea out of my mind. I pray about it, see if it is an idea that lies within scriptural guidance and in line with what Scripture teaches. I will then usually ask some advice from people I trust and respect to get their insights and counsel. Then, slowly but surely, I will end up finally doing it.

This particular idea, though, took a lot more "coaxing" from the Lord, because in the end, it was just an odd idea. "You're going to do what?" asked my friend Shane when I told him my new outreach idea. The look on his face let me know what he thought of it, but I was determined to go through with it, and like a good friend seeing his buddy getting ready to make a fool of himself, he encouraged me and used very strategic wording to show me he would "support" me.

A little history to bring this whole idea into context: It had been a long couple of weeks of doing college outreach. I love speaking to college students, as they are usually very eager to talk and share their thoughts. But the previous few weeks had been a continual onslaught of postmodern humanistic interactions. It seemed like reasoning and logic were just continually being dismissed in my conversations with people. Contradictions were not a problem for them in their worldviews. It was extremely frustrating.

As I left the campus that day, I remember thinking about how I was tired of doing conversational evangelism, and that I wanted to just stand in the middle of the campus and preach the gospel. I wanted to go from apologist to evangelist. I wanted to just "cut to the chase" and get past all the superficial philosophical garbage that our secular institutions were feeding the masses. At the same time, college ministry must be done tactfully and wisely. We had been doing evangelism on that campus for years, and I did not want to burn any bridges in any way. Not to mention, there were some great Christian student ministries on campus and I did not want to compromise their standing with the decision makers by being a John the Baptist. No, I needed a strategy.

And then the picture entered my mind: a picture that made me wonder if I needed to be admitted to an asylum. But it came into my mind nonetheless. And like many of the pictures the Lord had placed in my mind over the years, it was coupled with a healthy tension of excitement and fear. The picture was of me standing in a boat, in the middle of the common green on the campus, with life preservers all around me. On the side of the boat were the words "Man Overboard," and I was preaching from the boat. On the stern of the boat was the name "U.S.S. Repentance."

That's right, the picture was of me in a boat, on the grass, with life jackets. I told you it was weird. "Where in the world are you going to get a boat?" Shane asked me.

"I have no idea."

"How are you going to transport the thing?" he continued.

"I have no idea."

"Can we even do that legally?"

"I have no idea."

Shane's questions were all great questions, and over the years questions like that are one of the reasons I had grown to appreciate Shane. He is a thinker, a planner, a logistics type of guy. I need people like Shane in my life to bring me back to reality at times. His questions were not asked in a "lack of faith" way, but in a "hey, let's think this idea through" way. I love how God brings people together that complement each other well, even if it causes tension.

So I began my search for a boat. And wouldn't you know it, a friend of mine happened to have an old twelve-foot fishing boat that had been collecting moss for years behind his barn. I told him my idea, and asked him if he would consider selling it to me. "Better than that," he replied, "I'll just give it to you if you can come and pick it up."

As my son always tells me, "Cheap is good, but free is better!" Next thing I knew I was on my way to pick up the boat. When I saw the boat, I knew it was the one we needed—old, tired-looking, full of moss and character. I'd clean it up and it would be as good as new. I brought it back to the YWAM campus and spent the afternoon power washing it. I then asked a girl from the campus who was gifted artistically if she could paint the words on the side and stern of it, and she was more than happy to do so.

During this whole process many people would pass by on the YWAM campus, stop and ask me what in the world the boat was for, and after I would tell them, they complimented me with a smile and a look that left me thinking that they thought I was out to lunch. Finally, the day arrived for me to bring the U.S.S. Repentance to the college campus. I called it her maiden voyage.

As Shane and I carried the boat through the campus to the common green area, we both felt unbelievably awkward and uncomfortable as people stopped and just stared. We put the boat down where we thought we could get the most foot traffic, and we placed the life jackets around the ground near the boat. Before I knew it Shane tapped me on the shoulder and said, "Well, I'll see you later. I'll be over there praying for you, bro." And like a good friend, he left me to the wolves.

So there I was, a forty-one-year-old guy, sitting in a boat surrounded by life jackets on a college campus. I remember praying, "Lord, this is crazy, but please, use this thing to bring people to you." I looked over and saw Shane talking to a young guy, and pointing over to me. He had told him something like, "You see that weird dude over there? Go and see what he is talking about."

The next thing I knew, this guy approached me and asked what in the world I was doing. I told him I was a Christian guy who wanted to share with people what Jesus did for me, and I wanted to use this boat as a metaphor of my story. I then asked him if he wanted to listen to my story, to which he replied, "Well, anyone crazy enough to do something like this is worth listening to. Sure, can I sit down in your boat while you tell me?"

I could not believe it. The very first person who approached us was not only interested, but he was sitting in the boat listening to my testimony which led to me sharing the gospel with him. The whole time, I knew Shane was praying. We had a great conversation, and about thirty minutes after we had put that weird-looking boat on the green, this young man was surrendering his life to Christ. He was the only person who stopped and talked to us that day.

I learned so much from that day. I learned that God will go to great lengths to reach those who are searching. I am still amazed that young man was the only person we talked to that day. All the work to simply get that boat may have been just for one person. I learned that when the Lord lays something on your heart, no matter how crazy it may sound, our job is to obey and trust. Oftentimes, to the world we may look like fools, but people appreciate sincerity, even when it looks weird.

I also learned that sometimes people are fickle. I tried to follow up with that young man many times, but never heard from him again. Did he truly get saved? Was it a genuine conversion? I think so. It sure seemed so. I learned that the only test of a true conversion is time. I also learned that to be childlike not only in our faith but also in our evangelism is a whole lot of fun.

Questions to Ponder

1. How urgent would you consider the gospel message to be in your life?

2. How does that sense of urgency compel or discourage you from sharing the gospel with others?

3. What could be a creative way that you can draw people to you with the sole intention of sharing the gospel with them?

Martin Luther Would Have Done It

I do not nullify the grace of God; for if righteousness comes through the Law, then Christ died needlessly. –
Galatians 2:21

Some days are just slow doing evangelism. Sam and I had spent the morning doing outreach in a park area, but had not had many conversations. We walked quite a bit, and we decided that we needed to warm up as it was a chilly spring day. We decided to go into a massive Catholic church.

I've always loved big old churches, so we went in and sat in the pews. It was quiet inside, beautifully adorned with statues, stained glass, and candles. As I sat on the wooden pew and heard it squeak, and smelt the musty smell of old hymnals in the air, I was immediately reminded of my Lutheran upbringing. The sun pierced through the colorful stained glass windows, and added to the little light that the many candles gave off inside the church. There were a few people in the pews, lifting their prayers to God in silence.

It was such a peaceful place, and when the big wooden doors closed against the noise from the outside street traffic, it was as if you stepped into a whole new realm of solitude and serenity. As we sat and silently prayed for the people who were in pews (and, to be honest, lengthened our "prayer time" to warm our feet and hands), I had a thought come to my mind that at first was a bit shocking. Like a lightning bolt out of nowhere, this thought flashed across my mind: *Go and share the gospel with the priest, Tim.*

I looked around and did not see any priest, but I did see that the confessionals were open. Thankfully, both of them had a red lighted sign above them saying "occupied." *Whew, I dodged that bullet*, I thought. I went back to warming myself and admiring the beauty of the church, when the thought flashed across my mind again, and again, and again.

Finally, I succumbed to what could not have been anything else than the nudging of the Holy Spirit, and I tapped Sam on the shoulder and told him my thoughts. "I think the Lord is asking me to go and share the gospel with the priest!" I was kind of hoping Sam would chuckle a bit, place his hand on my shoulder and try to reason with me on why that might not be a good idea. After all, a priest should already know the gospel.

Well, I was to be disappointed as Sam gave a big smile and said, "Amen, great idea, I will pray for you as you do."

As I looked back at the confessionals, I could see the lights were red and they were still occupied. "Well, maybe next time," I said. "The lights are still red." To my amazement, the moment I said the word "red," one of the signs above the confessional switched to green and said "unoccupied," and a man walked out. *It's now or never*, I thought.

So I stood up and began the walk toward the confessional. I had never been in a confessional before in my life. It was a foreign thing to me, being raised Protestant, but I knew the basic reason for them. As I began to approach the confessional, I had so many thoughts enter my mind to try to dissuade my decision. *Who are you to ask a priest, Tim? You're just being judgmental, Tim. How dare you think you have something the priest doesn't?*

The thoughts kept coming. I even remember having the funny thought that Martin Luther would have spoken to the priest! I was not going to share with the priest because he was Catholic, I was doing it because the Lord asked me to. I would've done the same thing in a Protestant church had the situation been reversed. I know many Jesus-loving Catholics, as I do many Jesus-loving Protestants. In the end, we are all individuals, and have to be looked at as such. I have followed Jesus long enough to know that the church one attends is no spiritual indicator. I have always been cautious of becoming the Pharisee, so I knew my heart was in the right place. But man, the spiritual warfare going on was intense in my mind. It was tangibly felt. I almost turned around and went back to the pew but found myself already entering the confessional, shutting the door and kneeling before the latticed wall that kept my face from being seen.

Since I had never been in a confessional, but had seen a lot of movies that had them in it, I started with the only thing I knew. "Good morning, Father, it has been forty-one years since my last confession, and I am forty-one years old, if that tells you anything. My first confession is that I come here today as a Christian man, who would like to simply ask you what you believe the gospel to be. I know it may be weird, but that is why I am here."

The priest paused a bit, then I heard him chuckle a bit, and respond, "Well, this is a first. You do know you're technically supposed to be Catholic to come into a confessional, right? But since you're not confessing any sin, I think it's fine." The priest was friendly and to the point. But the next twenty minutes were some of the saddest twenty minutes of my life in witnessing. As we talked about grace, forgiveness through Jesus on the cross, heaven and hell, and other points of the gospel, I could come to no other conclusion than that this priest did not know Christ.

Just to be clear on what I was hearing I asked him one last question. "Father, if you died today, do you think you would be in heaven or hell?"

His answer astounded me. "Nobody can know that for sure, but I know I have lived a good life, and have done good things for the cause of Christ, so I trust Him to judge me appropriately."

I went another step. "Thank you for answering my many questions; can I ask you one more?"

"Sure," he said.

"Do you believe that Jesus is the only way to heaven, and the only way for forgiveness of sins?"

His answer put the nail in the coffin of where he stood when he came to the exclusivity of Christ. "That's a complicated question, and I know that God loves all people, so it is kind of hard to imagine he only has one way, no?"

We talked a little bit more, and I thanked him for his time. As I left I shared the gospel with him clearly, and challenged him to trust in Jesus Christ alone, not in the church, not in his works, not in anything other than His righteousness given to us. As I left, my heart was grieved. How many people went to that priest every day to pour out their hearts, ask advice, or seek counsel... and he was misleading them in more ways than one.

I sat back down in the pew and shared with Sam what the priest said, and we spent the next few moments praying for him. As we walked out of that beautiful church, I pondered how ironic it was that this church looked so beautiful and majestic and yet, within its doors I met a person whose soul was empty and lost. I met a spiritual leader who was trusting in his own works for salvation, thus rejecting the grace and forgiveness offered in the righteousness of Christ.

I learned that many people who work in churches are still lost, in need of a Savior. I learned that in the end, we are all responsible for who we say Jesus is, and whether or not we trust in Him. I learned that oftentimes, the darkest places are within the beautiful walls of our churches.

Questions to Ponder

1. Sometimes, churches can be like spiritual graveyards. Why is this?

2. Is the Lord calling you to have a conversation with someone you would rather not? If so, what is keeping you from obeying God in this?

3. Many people sit in church for years, but have never heard the gospel. How should this challenge you to respond to someone who says they know the gospel because they go to church?

The Real World

For the weapons of our warfare are not of the flesh, but divinely powerful for the destruction of fortresses. – 2 Corinthians 10:4

As I sat and listened to the translator, I was surprised when she asked us if we would like to join the monks for lunch. We were with some of our interns doing one of our Temple Talks, in which we bring Christians to non-Christian places to have worldview discussions, and learn about other religions.

This particular day we were at a Buddhist temple in our city, and had just finished our typical time of hearing about Buddhism and asking questions about the Buddhist religion. Being surrounded by Buddha statues, smelling the incense in the air, sitting on the floor, and hearing the Thai language literally made you feel you were in another country. I always enjoyed our times talking to the monks here, even if it was through a translator who themselves spoke broken English.

As I looked all around at our interns, I asked them if they would like to have lunch and most of them said yes, so we politely accepted the invitation. Now, I had never eaten lunch with a Buddhist monk before, so this would be a first time for me as well. When we entered the room where we were to eat, the amount of food in the center of the room resembled a feast fit for a king. I was hungry, so this made me all the happier.

However, my hunger would have to wait awhile longer as we were told by the translator that we first must wait for the monks to eat, then eat after them.

"Before we eat, we will have the monks chant," said the translator. "The chants are done before each meal, and when they chant, they are inviting the spirits of others to join them in the meal." I immediately got an empty feeling in my stomach, and began to pray in my spirit. As I looked at the eyes of all our interns, I could tell they all were doing the same.

For a moment I felt badly that I was putting them into this situation, as I knew this would be, for many of them, their first time ever experiencing something this demonic. But, I figured if we are called to be light, we should go to the dark places! I guess I did not realize how dark the nice-looking, beautifully decorated, ornate, Buddhist temple would be. So before I knew it, the monks began their chants, and I kid you not, about ten seconds after they began to chant, the temperature of the room dropped, and you could feel a dark presence. We could not understand a single thing they were chanting, but in the spiritual realm we could feel a demonic presence.

Then, right in the middle of the chanting, the translator nudged me and whispered to me, "You see, the spirits are here with us...look at my arm." I looked at her arm and she had goosebumps all over and the little hairs of her forearm were sticking straight up. I did not know what to say, so I just nodded and continued to pray. After the chanting had stopped the weird feeling of coolness in the room left, and we then watched the monks eat for about twenty minutes, then we sat down for a great meal. We learned the monks are always served their food; they never cook. It is always brought to them by people, so there were about four or five ladies who prepared their meals for them.

The food was delicious, and our time with them was a mixture of awkward smiles, long pauses of silence due to the language barrier, and a lot of questions in my mind as to what I was about to eat, and whether or not any of our interns were freaked out about what happened during the chanting. I had no idea if they also felt the temperature drop, or felt the dark presence, but I was anxious to find out in our debrief time we would have afterward.

We finished up our meal, thanked them for their hospitality, and left. As we stood outside our vans I asked, "What did you guys think of that?"

One lady answered, "I thought it was fascinating, but it also was really creepy. This may sound weird, but when we were in the room and the monks were chanting, I felt the room get colder."

"Me too!" said another person. A third concurred. So it was true. Every one of us experienced the same thing. We ended our time together interceding for the souls of those monks and translators. I learned that day that the spiritual world is indeed more real than we want to admit. As a matter of fact, in a way, it is much more real than the material world before us. I learned that wonderful, kind human beings, like those monks, have no idea how Satan has blinded them and is using his demons to hide the truth from them. I learned that no matter how nice a building or person may look, without Christ, every person and place is in darkness.

I learned that the Holy Spirit is always with us, and not only that, He protects us from the darkness that surrounds us. I learned that when you bring the light of Christ into a dark place, things happen, even if they may be strange things. I am so grateful we have a God who came down to our level to serve us, unlike the monks who demand service from others. I learned that right next door to all of us, whether it be a home, a temple, or a person, the dark places need the light of the gospel. The only question we need to ask is: are we willing to bring it?

Questions to Ponder

1. What "dark" places are near you right now that you can be a light to?

2. Are you stuck in a "Christian bubble"? How can you get out of the bubble and engage the lost today?

3. How can you begin to build bridges with nonbelievers today?

The Room Was Silent

Making the most of your time, because the days are evil. – Ephesians 5:16

One of the facets of our evangelistic ministry has been a three-month program called the Outward Apologetics School. It was a great school, designed to bring together the mind of the apologist with the heart of the evangelist. Each session had great content, dynamic speakers, unique components, and an evangelistic focus grounded on sound biblical truth.

At the beginning of this school, we went downtown to bring the students out to do evangelism. It would be their first time doing street evangelism with our school, so we planned a debrief time in our office afterwards.

This particular afternoon went pretty typically, with lots of rejection and a few great conversations; the gospel was shared. Overall, it was pretty "status quo" for evangelism on the streets of Salem, Oregon. When we returned to our office for the debrief, I asked our students how their time was.

I was not surprised at all when some of them said they did not like it; others were a bit discouraged, others were indifferent. One even bluntly said he thought it was not very effective. The general sense I gathered from the students was that the afternoon was like a bowl of oatmeal with no add-ons...a bit bland, not too impressive, and nothing to get excited about. That's okay, as I appreciated the honesty of the students. I'd rather have honest students than ones that try to impress by being fake. To be honest, I was thinking along those lines as well. Yes, even a guy who does evangelism all the time can get bored with it.

As I was beginning to wrap up the debrief time, I realized we still had one more student who had not shared, a young man from India named Thomas. He was a very quiet, humble, introverted guy, so it was no shock that I almost forgot to hear his feedback. He was always one of the last people to speak up, but whenever he did, people listened. He was our only international student, as all the other students came from America.

"Thomas, I almost forgot you. How did today go for you?"

Do you ever have one of those moments when someone is asked a question, and there is a long pause, followed by a feeling of expectancy, like something great is about to be said? This was one of those moments.

As Thomas humbly lifted his head from looking at the floor to looking at all of us in the room, I noticed his eyes were a bit watery, and he seemed a bit choked up. You could tell he was really pondering my question, and his response. Then, like someone who had just seen their first sunrise, with a big smile and eyes full of tears, he answered, "This afternoon was the most amazing time of my life. This was one of the first times in my life I have been able to openly share the gospel without fear of being beaten or killed. I thank the Lord for giving me this opportunity today."

The room was silent. All of us present were speechless. There it was: the reality check of all reality checks, the perspective adjustment of all perspective adjustments, the wake-up call of all wake-up calls. I really did not know what to say, other than something like, "Wow, Thomas, thank you for sharing." He nodded his head and, just as if he had never mentioned a thing, went back to the quiet persona that so defined him.

My life has never been the same since that day. What I learned that day was that I had been in danger of taking the gospel for granted. I had been in danger of treating the greatest message in the world with apathy. I had been in danger of becoming complacent in my Christian witness and stale in my zeal to share the gospel. Thomas had something I needed; he had something we all needed, and everyone in that room knew it. He had an appreciation for the message, and an appreciation forged through real life experience that taught him the cost that came with sharing it.

Thomas went on to become a very close friend. He even joined our ministry full time, and is one of the most gifted evangelists I know. I thank the Lord for that day in that little office, when the room became silent because of the words and reflections of one of the most silent people I have ever known, but one whose witness and life speaks loudest of all of a Savior who saves, and a message that needs to be shared.

Questions to Ponder

1. How have you taken for granted the freedoms we have in this nation to share the gospel?

2. In what ways can silence actually be very effective in evangelism?

3. Are you good at keeping things in a healthy perspective, which results in action and gratitude?

The Slow Process of Salvation

The Lord is not slow about His promise, as some count slowness, but is patient toward you, not wishing for any to perish, but for all to come to repentance. – 2 Peter 3:9

If you were to be walking by and glance at the table, you would have thought you were in a weird New Age bookstore. Crystal balls, tarot cards, a Buddha statue, a statue of Mary, the Book of Mormon, a few books written by atheists, a pentagram, Mary Baker Eddy's *Key to the Scriptures*, and a Bible were just a few of the many different items on the table. A big red banner with the words "Take Your Pick" stood out in the student commons like a sore thumb.

Interested, curious students would approach to inquire what all the stuff was about. They were drawn to the table like bees to honey. Our "Take Your Pick" table is one of my favorite outreaches that we typically use on college campuses. We place all these things on a table and ask students what their spiritual beliefs are, and in the process many doors are opened to share the gospel. It is a fantastic outreach, and always produces fascinating conversations.

As we sat and talked with students, one young man approached the table and I asked him if he had a moment for a conversation. With a kind, polite smile, after glancing at the time, he said, "Sure, I've got time before my next class." He sat down, which immediately told me that our conversation was going to be longer than the typical thirty second fly-by. He introduced himself as Galen, a drafting student.

From the get-go I knew this guy was a very smart person, and a thinker. After a few moments of feeling each other out in the flow of conversation, he said to me, "This is actually really weird. But I have been pondering God, faith, and all this stuff a ton lately." The Lord had sent us his Nicodemus for the day. I asked him some thought-provoking questions, heard his responses, and the conversation was very positive and interactive. I love when witnessing becomes a two-way conversation rather than just me talking, or just me listening. Galen seemed to know how to carry a conversation very well, and he was very open to asking questions and being asked questions.

After a bit of time, he began to open up about his personal story. When God is working on a person's heart it usually goes that way. During the first part of the conversation people stick to the topic we are discussing, but then as the conversation continues, they begin to open up and allow you into their personal lives. This is where it is exciting to see how the Holy Spirit is tilling the hearts of people.

"My mom is very Christian," he said. "She goes to church all the time, reads her Bible, and I know she has been praying for me forever." Out of curiosity, I asked him which church his mom attended. "It's a small church in South Salem."

Intrigued and curious because I myself attend a small church in South Salem, I asked him, "What small church in South Salem?"

"It's called Way of Life Fellowship."

"Really? Well, you're never going to guess where I go to church," I said to him.

While shaking his head, with a big grin he said, "You're gonna tell me that you go to Way of Life Fellowship."

"Yep." I answered. Not only did I go to the same church his mom went to, but I actually knew his mom. The "sovereign stars" were aligning for Galen. After our conversation, we set a date to meet weekly.

That day, I called my pastor and told him the story. Unbeknownst to me, my pastor knew Galen well, and had been praying for his salvation for a long time, just as Galen's mother had been. "Keep praying for him, I am going to be meeting with him weekly." I told my pastor. Over the next few weeks, Galen and I met for coffee. We covered all sorts of theological terrain in our talks, and it was so clear God was doing a work in him. We became good friends. He was brutally honest in his faith journey, and had not come to the point where he wanted to fully trust in Christ. I gave him a copy of my favorite book, *Pilgrim's Progress*, which to my surprise he devoured quickly. We talked a lot about the book, and along with reading the Bible, I could see the Holy Spirit working on Galen's heart and mind.

Galen then began to come to church. Week after week, he came faithfully, full of sincere questions. Over the span of a few months I, along with many others, continued to pray for Galen.

Then, one Sunday afternoon my pastor called me. "Hey, I didn't see you at church this morning, so I had to call you." Yes, I had skipped church that morning. "Galen came up to me today after service and said he was ready to commit his life to Jesus. He gave his life to Christ today." I asked my pastor all the details of how the conversation went, and I immediately gave Galen a phone call.

Since that day, Galen has literally grown in his faith by leaps and bounds. He is active in our church, involved in Bible study, and is presently doing our evangelism internship. After knowing Jesus for a year, he approached me and said that it was time for him to start sharing with others what Jesus had done for him.

Galen is a testimony of how God uses all sorts of ways to reach an individual. His mom had been praying for him. Our church had been praying for him. I had been praying for him. Through many conversations over coffee, the Lord allowed me to plant various seeds. Through a classic book like *Pilgrim's Progress*, the Holy Spirit continued to till the rough, hard soil of Galen's heart and mind. Imagine if John Bunyan could have realized how his allegory he wrote from prison would aid in the process of salvation for Galen. Through God's perfect timing, He allowed our pastor to reap the harvest that Sunday after church.

Sometimes salvation in an individual is a process. Layer after layer, Galen had his spiritual blinders removed over time. For some it is a quick, once-and-done thing, but for Galen, the patience of the Lord to reach one soul shines forth brightly. Galen had a slow process of salvation that resembled an old-fashioned clock, filled with a number of different moving parts, all working together for the same purpose. All those moving parts in Galen's story were all working together to see this kind young man come to know the One who saved him from his sin.

Questions to Ponder

1. Think about your salvation testimony. How was God moving in your life before you were even a Christian?

2. In what ways can you plant seeds into the lives of others who are seeking truth?

3. How do different salvation stories glorify God?

Unworthy to Share

*Wretched man that I am! Who will set me free from
the body of this death? – Romans 7:24*

It had been one of those mornings. In fact, it had been
one of those weeks. I'm talking about those times
when my life reflects more of a selfish toddler than a
believer. My heart, soul, and mind were just stressed
out, short-tempered, and frustrated. I can't really recall
the reasons why, but I was just in the "spiritual
dumps." I was not reading the Bible, I was ignoring
prayer and time with the Lord, and the fruits of that
could be seen in how I was acting with others. My
family has seen these times in my life, to my shame:
those times when Dad is "not doing well."

That particular morning, as I headed downtown to our
office I thought, *I do not want to go do evangelism
today. I don't feel like it. I don't really care about
telling others about Jesus today. Send someone else,
Lord. Why don't others get off their tails and share the
gospel? Why do I have to always be the one reminding
people?* Self-pity and self-righteousness took root. Then
doubts began to creep in. *Tim, who are you to go and
tell people about Jesus? Just look at you; you're not
necessarily a model Christian, are you, Tim? And what
about those harsh words you said to your wife? Not to
mention, your impatience with your children?
Remember the bad thoughts you had the other day?
And you are a bit prideful, aren't you, Tim?*

It was as if Satan was launching all the arrows in the world at me, and they were hitting the chinks in my armor. I pulled up to the office and took a deep breath, complained a bit more, and then got out and "put on my good Christian face." It was summer, so we were going to the market in our city to do conversational evangelism. As we set up, all I wanted to do was go home. I truly did not want to be there. Yes, I have those days. More than I would like to admit, to be honest. *Well, Tim, you can soldier through this for the next few hours,* was the thought that came to my mind.

Thankfully, I was not facilitating a group, so I could kind of "lazy" my way through the morning. As I stood there, the attacks from the sales pitch of the enemy continued on, and I was actually buying what he was selling. I had no business being out there telling others about Jesus. I was a hypocrite. I should just go home. That was the frame of mind I was in as an elderly lady and her husband approached me. They were followed by four young teenagers. I was correct in my assumption that it was a grandpa and grandma with their grandkids, as the lady introduced herself and explained they were spending the day with her four grandkids. She was interested in the table we had set out, which simply asked the question, "What do you believe about the Bible?"

"I'd like you to ask my grandkids this question," she said. As she said that, she gave me a quick wink. Years of ministry had taught me what that meant. She was a believer and she wanted her grandkids to hear what we had to say. I can't explain it, but sometimes you just know when someone is a follower of Jesus simply by a look they give you, or a thing they say, or as in this case, a gesture they give you. The conversation immediately went deep with the four teens. They were all brothers and sisters. Clearly, Grandma couldn't care less about the awkwardness of putting her grandkids on the spot. "Tell them what you believe," she said to me.

I remember feeling a bit bad for the teens as they obviously were forced into a conversation, but I did my best to connect with them, and in the end shared the gospel. They admitted they were just going through the motions of what was expected of them from their parents and church. Their grandma had a tear in her eye. It was a sincere, powerful time. "You know, I have kids too. I understand the tension of trying to please your parents, and 'do the right thing.' But the reality is, guys, you are responsible for your decision of what you do with Jesus. Not your parents, or even your grandparents. Each of you will stand before God one day, and the Lord is not going to ask you if you did what your parents asked you to do, or believed what they believed. He is going to ask you what you did with His Son Jesus. That decision is something only you can make. Your grandparents obviously love you, but behind their love is their desire to spend eternity with you guys, and that only can happen when you guys trust in Christ as they have. Does that make sense?"

What happened next was one of the most impactful times of witnessing I have ever had. The four teens looked at each other, and right there on the spot, decided that they wanted to place their full trust in Jesus Christ. They all joined hands, and right there in the market, holding the hands of their grandparents, they surrendered their lives to Jesus and decided to make their faith in Him their own. As we ended our prayer, their grandmother gave me a big hug, and in a grandmotherly way held my cheeks, looked into my eyes, and said, "Thank you so much for being here today, young man. Thank you. We have been praying for our grandkids for years, and they were answered today by you being here. I can't wait to tell their parents, and you have my word we will hold them accountable to the profession of faith they made today." Praying grandparents are powerful instruments of the Lord for salvation.

With that, they had to be on their way. As they walked away, I was filled with awe and shame at the same time. Awe that four teens had just surrendered their lives to Christ. Shame in that I had the privilege of being the person to "lead" them to Jesus in spite of the state of my sinful, selfish heart. That lady had no idea the thoughts I had been having that morning. If she had, she probably would have passed us by!

Why God allowed me that amazing experience, I have no idea, but He did. I sure did not deserve it, considering the type of guy I was. I learned that He will work through our imperfections to reach people. Many times, I get so focused on myself that I fail to focus on others. I did not want to be out there that day. I wanted to be selfish and just go home.

I learned that God will work through our own brokenness. Most of all, I learned that there is no such thing as being "good enough" to share the gospel with others. The gospel drives us to actually show us our imperfections, and that we need a Savior. Lord, help me never to think that I have attained the status of being worthy to share the gospel. For in my unworthiness, the grace of Christ shines brightest.

Questions to Ponder

1. What lies has the enemy put into your heart or mind to keep you from sharing the gospel?

2. Why is it important to know that God can use you for His glory even when you may not feel like you deserve it?

3. What is the difference between guilt-driven evangelism and gratitude-driven evangelism?

When God Answers Specific Prayers

But this kind does not go out except by prayer and fasting. – Matthew 17:21

"Here he comes again, Tim," said my friend Ryan. I looked across the street and there was Roger, coming right toward us. Hunched over, with long straggly hair, his guitar and backpack over his side, he was fast approaching us.

The scene was all too familiar. I immediately became tense, took a deep breath, and asked the Lord to give me grace, compassion, and even prayed for safety. "How are you doing, Roger?" Ryan asked.

Without waiting a second, Roger blurted out a novel of obscenities, and spit on the ground next to us. "That's not nice, Roger," I replied, but it was of no use; he was on another one of his "benders" of cursing us out. As he gave us his standard farewell with a middle finger, he walked away.

"What are we going to do about this guy?" I asked Ryan. Roger had become a serious problem for us. At first, it was just an occasional annoying conversation where he would go on a rant about how he was the only one who had the true "religion." He was the leader of a small cult in our city that believed you could only understand the truth if you spoke Hebrew. He would send his cronies to disturb us, but they were all usually pretty kind. It was Roger who was the real problem.

For weeks, he had intentionally begun to disturb us on the streets. He would stand a few feet away and just mock us, and mock the Lord. The things that he would say were terrible. It was in every way an uncomfortable, awkward, and frustrating situation. Recently, though, something had become very different in how he went about his mocking. It had become more intentional, more aggressive, and darker. There was a hatred in his voice, and an anger in his face, that had not been there before. When Roger approached, we could literally feel the spiritual atmosphere of the area shift. It may sound weird, but his eyes were not human eyes. It was a demonic presence staring at us.

So, for a while, we dealt with Roger like you would deal with a leaky faucet—we put up with it. But then it all came to a head one day when I was out with some high school students and he said some appalling stuff to a girl who was with us. "Roger, get out of here. I'll call the cops if you don't. You can't say that type of stuff, not ever. Get away now," I told him.

Roger took a step toward me and then said something I will never forget. "I'm going to kill you. If you show up here tomorrow, I am going to stab you with a knife and kill you."

There was nothing within me that did not believe Roger. He was serious, and it frightened me, but I had to "keep it together" for the sake of the students who were with me. Thankfully, he walked away.

After we ended the day with the students, I told Ryan about what happened. "What do we do? I'm done with this guy! Do we call the cops? Do we show up tomorrow? He is a psycho. We can't keep having him do this stuff. That was a literal life threat." I vented my frustrations to Ryan, and awaited his response. Ryan has always been a friend who I really admire in many ways. He can build anything with his hands, and is a true servant, the type of guy who will give you the shirt off his back if needed. But what I've always appreciated about him more than anything is his spiritual perspective and godly counsel on things, and his response was true to that.

"We need to pray and fast for Roger. That's what we need to do." Well, what a novel idea! Pray and fast. Do what the Bible says!

I chuckled and said, "I was kind of hoping you would say something different. Something like, let's call the cops, or let's just switch locations where we do outreach to avoid him."

But Ryan was right, and I knew it. I remember going home that evening truly bothered by what Roger said, but convicted and compelled to do what Ryan had suggested. I did not tell my wife about Roger's words, as I did not want her to worry about me. To be honest, I was a bit scared as to what would happen to me if I did go back the next day, but after prayer and committing the day to the Lord I went back the next morning. Ryan and I met up, prayed, and did not see Roger the whole day!

That's odd, we both thought. God was beginning to do something. We began to pray specific prayers for God to either remove Roger, save Roger, or distract Roger from interrupting us or even hurting us. About a week after we began to pray, we were on the corner one day and we saw Roger walking down the sidewalk when, out of nowhere, a police car pulled up next to him. The next thing we knew, Roger was getting into the police car.

Ryan and I looked at each other in shock. Roger had been picked up by the cops and was no longer allowed in the downtown area, which happened to be right where we always were. God had answered our prayers.

I learned that the spiritual world is just as real as the physical. I always knew that, but when you stare into the eyes of a demonically possessed person, over and over, it becomes real. I learned that there is a dark, evil, demonic world out there that does not want the gospel to go forth, and when we proclaim it, we must expect adversity. I learned that God's Word is true. When we pray and fast, things happen. I learned that it is easy to try to solve problems without ever seeking the Lord in how to solve them.

I'm so glad Ryan challenged us to pray and fast for a person I honestly could not stand at the time. This was God's answer for our problem with Roger. I learned that Jesus died for people like Roger, and that I was in danger of having my heart become hard towards him. Lastly, I learned that when we pray specifically, many times the Lord answers specifically. Sometimes it's even in the form of a police car.

Questions to Ponder

1. Is God asking you to love and be patient with a person in your life right now whom you don't feel deserves it? What should your attitude be?

2. Jesus assumes that His followers pray...and fast. Is fasting a part of your spiritual disciplines? Why or why not?

3. In what ways are you staying sensitive to the spiritual world that is around us?

When the Fruit is Ripe for the Taking

Then they came to the valley of Eshcol and from there cut down a branch with a single cluster of grapes; and they carried it on a pole between two men, with some of the pomegranates and the figs. – Numbers 13:23

It was a cold, rainy day, the type of Northwest day that I had grown so accustomed to but never enjoyed. I remember the rain falling on me and asking myself, *Why in the world am I out here today?* That type of thought often comes into my mind here in Oregon, where it is so damp I usually have to take a shower to dry off. It was a typical day of standing in front of our local shopping mall, asking people if they had a minute for a conversation, in which we would then share the gospel.

This morning was slow in terms of people stopping to talk, and although I usually have someone with me, I was alone this particular day. I spotted a young guy in a black sweatshirt approaching me at a rather quick pace. As he crossed the street I noticed his hood was up over his head, and his head was drooping to the ground, but his eyes were set on me. His shoulders swaggered back and forth, almost like a boxer does on his way to the ring. I was not sure what to think, as it is rare for anyone to approach with that much intention and determination. Usually I have to stop people and interrupt them to tell them about Jesus, but it was clear from the way this guy was approaching me that would not be necessary.

"Hey, my name is Timo." he said. As he introduced himself, I noticed his face was pale, thin, and he looked sad and even a bit concerned. He looked really worried about something. "So, this may sound crazy to you, but a few weeks back I spoke to a guy next to one of your signs, and he asked me about the Bible, and if I knew anything about it. We had a pretty cool conversation. Anyway, that started me on an intense quest to figure out the answer to that, and I have not had any peace since that day."

He then shared how he had recently moved to Salem from Las Vegas to try and get away from a lifestyle of drugs, immorality, and essentially a path that he had the good sense to try and get out of. As he shared, I thought that it was pretty cool that he had obviously had a conversation with my friend Ryan a few weeks back. I was getting ready to ask him a question, when all of a sudden, with a concerned look on his face he blurted out, "What do I need to do to get to heaven?"

He could not have been more serious, and I could not have been more surprised. I remember thinking to myself, *Did he really just ask that?* Usually, that type of question comes after countless long, hard conversations over coffee with someone, and could take weeks, months, and years of prayers and persistence, but not in this case. To add to that, what caught me off guard was that I literally just met the guy a minute before, and here, on a cold rainy corner, he was asking me arguably the most important question a person could ask! Timo was not joking at all. His face had sincerity and desperation written all over it. If God could have thrown a softball over home plate to knock out of the park with the message of the gospel, this was it.

After recovering from the shock of his openness and question, I simply shared the gospel with him, and right there in front of the mall he repented of his sins and accepted Christ as his Savior. Timo and I may have just been going about our daily business, but the Lord had decided this would be the right place for Timo and the right time. Or to be more biblically correct, the right place at the God time.

What I learned that day was that the conviction of sin will lead people to the cross. Timo was desperate for a Savior, because when he read the Bible, it became clear to him that he needed one, and that it was Jesus.

The other thing I learned was that God is in the business of saving people, and sometimes He blesses us with the privilege to be the person who sees a sinner repent and surrender to Him. Sometimes the fruit is so ripe and ready to fall from the tree, all you have to do is put out your hand. I did nothing that day other than step into the work that the Holy Spirit had already begun in this young man's life. God was already moving in Timo's life, and for His reasons and His reasons alone, he allowed me the privilege of being the one to lead Him to Jesus at that moment. Timo was ripe fruit prepared by the Lord for salvation. I often think of how it was my friend Ryan's initial conversation with Timo that was the spark that started it all. God loves to use all of us for His purposes, and what a joy to see how He uses us for different things, at different times. Sometimes we are the planters, sometimes the sowers, sometimes the reapers.

Timo is now a very passionate follower of Jesus. He was baptized, became involved with a great church, got a great job, got married, had some kids, and even did one of our evangelism internships. He has become a good friend, and a stable Christian presence in our city. He is also a pretty good rapper and one of the most vulnerable, sincere guys I know. I thank the Lord for that cold rainy day in front of the mall. I thank Him that I was able to simply put out my hands and see the fruit of His work drop into them.

Questions to Ponder

1. Why is it important to understand in evangelism that it is God who saves people?

2. Do you consider yourself to be a planter, waterer, or harvester when it comes to evangelism?

3. Why is it important that we always talk about sin when sharing the gospel with others?

When the Trail Goes Cold

And He spoke many things to them in parables, saying,
"Behold, the sower went out to sow." – Matthew 13:3

The little town of McMinnville, Oregon is a quiet, quaint place. It has a kind of Norman Rockwell feel to it with old-fashioned window front stores and wide streets. However, in May the place turns into one of the weirdest places on the planet as it hosts the annual "UFO Festival." That's right: each year, thousands of UFO enthusiasts gather for three days in this little town. It is basically like three days of Halloween, as thousands of people are dressed up as aliens, space creatures, and monsters, and have their vehicles morphed into flying saucers on wheels. It is an exciting, fun time, and just about everything you can imagine is there. Seminars, activities, games, events, and concerts are all part of the weekend.

Over the years, I have observed four groups of people. There are the truly serious UFO enthusiasts who believe, heart, soul, and mind, in extraterrestrial life. These are the ones that put on seminars, sell their books, are sometimes into conspiracy theories, and usually walk around with a look on their face that at any moment the mother ship could come for us all.

The second group is the people who have food and merchandise booths. The third group is the people who heard about the event and came to check it out, just wanting to see something different, and have a good time. The fourth group are those involved in the occult: palm readers, tarot card readers, "spiritual healers," and the like.

It was at this event that we went to do our "Great Invasion" outreach. We set up a tent with a big banner all decked out to fit the theme of UFOs and space, that said, "What if the Great Invasion Already Happened?" We then set out some tables with things like crystal balls, Bibles, the Koran, a Buddha statue, and a host of other religious and spiritual symbols to draw attention.

From the moment we set up our tent, people approached us and wanted to talk. Without exaggeration, there was a lineup of people for the next six hours. We had hundreds of witnessing opportunities and were able to share the gospel all day long. Since there were about twenty of us only a few could be under the tent, so the rest split up into groups and mingled with the crowd, witnessing and doing prayer walks. It was amazing to see, all over the festival, Christians sharing the gospel with people.

After walking around in the crowd, it was my shift at the tent. As I ducked into the tent, my buddy Cole sat there in a chair. "How's it been going?" I asked him.

With a huge sigh and an exhausted look on his face, Cole said, "Amazing, but I literally can't talk to one more person. My brain is fried. I have not stopped sharing the gospel for hours. I'm a baked man. But it has been so amazing, Tim. Usually we have to go out of our way to get people to talk to us, but today, it's just the opposite!" Cole was right; the Lord was doing something that day.

For the remainder of the day we had opportunities like crazy to share the gospel; it literally never stopped. One after another, people came to the tent. What was crazy is our booth was next to a palm reader! You could feel the spiritual warfare going on. I decided to take another walk and give my brain a rest. There are few things more exhausting than witnessing for hours on end, as it zaps you of everything. (At least it does for me, but that might be because my mental capacity resembles that of a snail, but that's beside the point.)

I decided to stop at one of our corners where we had a table set up to see how the others were doing, when all of a sudden I found myself in a fantastic conversation with a young man named Ryan. He was a college student and had loads of questions about what we were doing, about God, science, and many topics. We talked for an hour, and I was able to share the gospel with him a few times. "Man, this has been a fascinating conversation Tim. I'd love to get together again. Can I get your number?" As an evangelist, this is the question you dream about. It's the Cadillac of questions. The big one. It makes the hours of rejections and naysaying worth it.

"Absolutely, Ryan. Let's do it." I gave him my number, took his number, and we parted ways. *What a fantastic day*, I thought to myself. So many people heard the gospel today, and I even got a follow-up with someone. I went home exhausted, yet happy. A few days passed and I gave Ryan a call. I was excited to set up a time to meet for coffee. He picked up the phone. "Hey, Ryan, it's Tim...the weird Christian guy you ran into last week." Nothing wrong with being honest; I am a bit weird. "I was wanting to know when we could go out for coffee and continue our discussion?"

There was an odd, long pause on the phone. "Hey, Tim, thanks for calling...but you know, I've been talking to my family and some friends of mine, and I think they gave me the answers I need, so I don't think it's necessary." Now, I knew his family were not believers, as he mentioned that to me in our conversation, so this was not good that he "found" the answers he needed from them. I politely asked him what conclusions he came to, but he dismissed the question and said he needed to go. And just like that, our conversation ended. The trail had gone cold.

Sometimes we just can't explain how or why people do the things they do. I honestly thought Ryan was someone who was searching, and I honestly thought the Lord was opening a door, but that door was shut. Or at least from my perspective, it had shut. Maybe the Lord got to Ryan another way. I learned that we will be disappointed often when we witness to others. Mankind is fickle, and can be tossed by many winds that come their way.

Amidst my disappointment with Ryan, I learned that when Christians intentionally invade their world with the gospel, God honors that. So many seeds were planted in the hearts of people that day, and I thank the Lord for that. I learned that in the end, God draws people to Him in His timing, and how He wants. What a blessing to be able to be a part of that...even when the trail goes cold.

Questions to Ponder

1. What festivals or other events are in your area that you could use for evangelism?

2. How do you measure the success of evangelism?

3. How can Jesus' parable of the seeds landing on different soils be an encouragement to you during evangelism?

Epilogue

It is said that every good story must come to an end, and so here we find ourselves at the end point of this one. I hope that you have enjoyed these stories, and thank you for allowing me the privilege to share them with you. Maybe some spoke to you in a way that was more memorable than others. Maybe some challenged you. Maybe some made you ask yourself tough questions. Maybe some were simply reminders for you. Hopefully, all of them compel you to share the gospel with others.

You see, these stories are not just remembrances of the past, they are only the beginnings of the continuing work of God in the lives of all the people involved. God's story continues and we all are a part of that.

I was trying to think of how to end a book that is a collection of stories. Being the innovative guy that I am, I decided to end it with a story.

Back in college, I spent a summer working at a Christian camp as a guide on an old-fashioned wagon train. Yes, you heard it correctly, an old-fashioned wagon train. It was my dream job, to be honest, as I had always wanted to be a "cowboy" who lived under the stars and roamed the open range. It was an amazing summer, as my days were spent on horseback, my nights were spent sleeping under the stars, and I was able to live my cowboy dream.

Aside from being on horseback eight hours a day, I was also in charge of leading Bible studies for the young high school kids that came through week after week. Now, that may sound cool, but there was one major problem...I was not a Christian. You heard that right. I was working at a Christian camp as a Bible camp counselor, but was not a Christian.

I won't go into detail about how I was able to get that job, but to this day I know it was the hand of the Lord drawing me to Him. And that came about in three main ways. The first was that I had a lot of time to reflect on life, sitting on a horse for eight hours a day. As I looked at the stars at night, I began to wonder about life, death, and my purpose? I simply spent a lot of time thinking of my life at twenty years old.

The second was, I felt very guilty leading Bible studies; to be honest, I had no idea what I was doing or what any of the stuff meant. The Bible started to actually bother me a bit, because I realized I was not living the way it laid out for me. As a matter of fact, I was the proverbial hypocrite, as I would lead Bible studies with people during the week, but then spend the weekend living in the ways of the world. And trust me, I was good at that.

The third thing that happened to me was in the form of a confrontation. It was on the weekend, and I was doing my typical thing of drinking a lot of beer and having "a good time." I was with some other staff who were also not following the Lord, and we were minding our own business when all of a sudden a young girl who worked at another camp walked up to me, pointed her finger in my face and said, "You're not a Christian, Tim. You're a fake. Why in the world are you doing this stuff? How can you call yourself a Christian?"

I remember it felt like time stood still. Inside I knew she was right. But I did the classic thing and told her to chill out, and I brushed her off. Thankfully, she did that in love and grace and did not keep pestering me. I went to bed that night bothered by what she said, not just because it was embarrassing, but because I knew she was right.

That fall, as I went back to college, not a day went by that I did not think of what she said. One day, after many more stories of God's prompting and drawing, I knelt down in my room and surrendered my life to Jesus Christ fully.

You see, the stained glass sidewalk in my story took many forms. It was a mix of God's revealing Himself through creation, the conviction of His word, and the boldness of a person to confront me with truth. All of those and many other stories were stained glass sidewalks for me. I look back and am humbled at the amazing grace and patience of God in my story. That is why I decided to close this book with part of my story, because my life is completely a gift of His grace that I desire to use for His glory and purposes. May you, dear reader, do the same with the life He has given you.

WHAT IS OVERBOARD BOOKS

Overboard Books publishes quality books that are designed to assist in getting Christians overboard — out of the boat. It's the publishing arm of Overboard Ministries, whose mission is based on Matthew 14. In that chapter we find the familiar story of Jesus walking on water while His disciples were in a boat. It was the middle of the night, the water was choppy and Jesus freaked out His followers who thought He was a ghost. When they realized it was Him, Peter asked to come out to Him on the water, and he actually walked on top of the water like Jesus.

But what truly captivates me is the thought of the other eleven disciples who remained in the boat. I've often wondered how many of them questioned that move in the years to come? How many of them wished they hadn't stayed in the boat but had instead gone overboard with Peter? Overboard Ministries aims to help Christians get out of the boat and live life for Christ out on the water where He is. We hope and pray that each book published by Overboard Ministries will stir believers to jump overboard and live life all-out for God, full of joy, and free from the regret of "I wish I had…"

What we do

Overboard Ministries emerged in the Spring of 2011 as an umbrella ministry for several concepts my wife and I were developing. One of those concepts was a book ministry that would help other Christian authors get published. I experienced a lot of frustration while passing my first manuscript around. I kept getting rejection letters that were kindly written, but each echoed the same sentiment: "We love this book. If you were already a published author, we would love to publish it." They were nice letters, but that didn't make the rejection any easier or the logic less frustrating.

Out of that came the audacious idea to start our own "publishing company." I put that in quotes because I want people to know a couple of things. First of all, we're not a traditional publishing company like most people envision when they hear the name. We don't have a printing press in our garage, and we don't have a marketing team. Basically, we're a middle-man who absorbs most of the cost of publishing in order to help you get published, while making sure the majority of profits end up in your pocket, not ours.

Our desire is to keep costs to a bare minimum for each author. (As of this writing, there is only a minimal contract fee when your manuscript is accepted.) We provide resources and ideas to help authors work on marketing, while also providing the editor and graphic design artist at our expense. We subcontract out the printing, which speeds up the time it takes to move from final draft to bound book. Since we don't have much overhead we can keep our expenses low, allowing seasoned authors, or first-time authors like me, the opportunity to profit from their writing. This makes it possible for authors to publish more books while continuing in their current jobs or ministries.

Contact us
If you are interested in other books or learning about other authors from Overboard Books, please visit our

website at **www.overboardministries.com** and click on the "Overboard Books" link. If you are an author interested in publishing with us, please visit our site and check out the "Authors" tab. There you will find a wealth of information that will help you understand the publishing process and how we might be a good fit for you. If we're not a fit for you, we'll gladly share anything we've learned that might be helpful to you as you pursue publishing through other means.

Thank you
Thanks for supporting our work and ministry. If you believe this book was helpful to you, tell someone about it! Or better yet, buy them a copy of their own! We completely depend on word-of-mouth grassroots marketing to help spread the word about Overboard Ministries and its publications. Please share our website with others and encourage them to purchase the materials that will help them live "overboard" lives for Christ.

May God bless you as you grab the side of boat, take a deep breath…and jump onto the sea!

Joe Castaneda
Founder, Overboard Ministries

Made in the USA
Columbia, SC
31 May 2021